THE MARCH OF ELEVEN MEN

THE MARCH OF
ELEVEN MEN

By

FRANK S. MEAD

THE BOBBS-MERRILL COMPANY

PUBLISHERS   INDIANAPOLIS

2 70T
M 461
93931

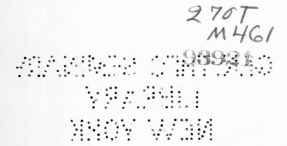

PRESS OF
BRAUNWORTH & CO., INC.
BOOK MANUFACTURERS
BROOKLYN, N. Y.

To
JUDY

CONTENTS

PROLOGUE

THE modern man is a tired individual. Especially is he tired if he is still a seeker after truth in things religious. He has been buried in a deluge of cynicism, caught in the noisy barrage of a modern writing which insists that religion is useless, the refuge of the coward and the moron, the ghost of a dead past. He is unconsciously the victim of those who have created the new, the great, the popular American indoor sport of stone-throwing at everything and anything Christian. Everett Dean Martin says that religion is primarily a "defense mechanism." Llewelyn Powys says even more flatly: "We have pretended long enough. Christianity is but a dream of savagery and pitifulness."

Christians are blamed for failing to stop the last war, and for going to it: pacifists or warriors, they are equally at fault. They are censured for tolerating a cruel and unjust economic order, where suffer and die their fellow men; they are roundly abused for "butting in" in the affairs of factory, office, mine and shop. They are scolded for talking of jasper paradise in the next world while they neglect the sins and crimes of the present one, and they are vilified for "mixing religion with politics."

That criticism has been overdone. The canvas of the Christianity-hater is topheavy and out of proportion

with colors too gaudy and untrue. There are other
truths which have been neglected, other colors left dry-
ing in the tubes of the artists. When all the mistakes
and shortcomings of Christianity have been accounted
for and properly advertised, there still remains the fact
that it has been the most vital of all influences playing
on the moral, spiritual and social problems of the race;
there still remains the fact that the Church started with
eleven men, and to-day numbers over five hundred millions.

Institutional Christianity, probably because it has
grown so fast, has made mistakes. But inasmuch as mistakes come easy to institutions and to individuals alike,
it would seem quite as unfair to condemn one as the
other; as unfair to seek the destruction of an institution
for its mistakes as it would be to destroy a man for drunk-
enness. A mother can not see her baby grow inch by
inch and year by year, to the full stature of a man; yet
she does not kill the baby because she can not "see."

We write neither a history of nor an apology for the
Church. We would paint no rosy half-true picture of
her steady march to power or of her constant, never-
mistaken influence for God. We would tell another
story: the story of the march of the spirit of Christ
across the corridors of time. We would trace some of
the great influences of that spirit, left in the keeping of
eleven men and still singing in the heart of the Church,

on the mind and manners of every age of men since Calvary.

The spirit of Jesus is the hub of history—the great central fact about which have gone whirling the currents and the movements of time. It has been the dynamo of human progress, the leaven working in historical process to produce much of the benefits and glories of modern life.

The "modern crisis" of Christianity is nothing new. It has always been face to face with a crisis. Thomas Paine sentenced it to death some hundred years ago, but it survived, to wield an influence respected by statesmen and pedagogues alike. Voltaire gave it but a few short years to live, but it grew from two to five hundred millions within a century after he had found his grave. Nero and Diocletian tried fire and the lions, and the rabble of slaves they persecuted snatched the scepter of power from their sons. Longinus, the centurion, reported to Caiaphas that the man Jesus was dead and sealed in a tomb. But . . .

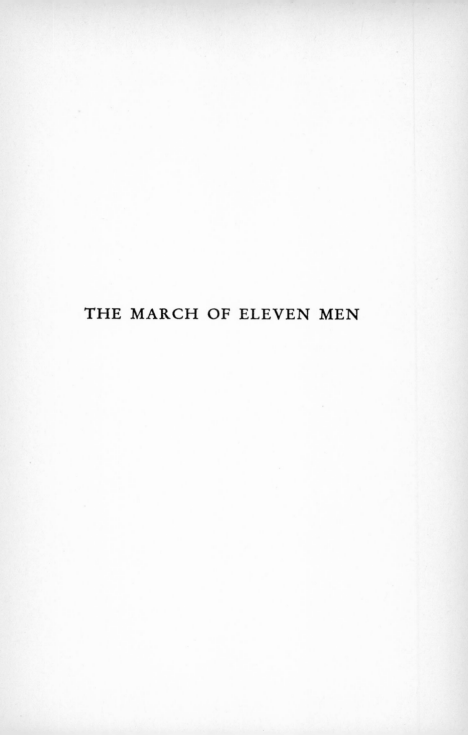

THE MARCH OF ELEVEN MEN

THE MARCH OF ELEVEN MEN

CHAPTER I

THE MARCH BEGINS

LONGINUS was mad: red-mad, at everything and
every one in sight. He hated this Jerusalem, these Jews.
He, a fighting centurion, sent to guard a lot of detest-
able foreigners while other centurions were marching
with their legions on the other side of the world! He
kicked out furiously at every stone in his path, mumbling to himself that he wished he might be kicking Jews.
He even snarled at the innocent morning sun just then
coming up over the city wall, for the rising of the sun
reminded him that he must hurry: three Jews were
waiting to be crucified. Longinus hated crucifixions.
Why couldn't criminals be matched like gladiators, one
against the other, as they were in Rome? Rome! How
he wanted to be there! Homesick, disgusted, half asleep
after a night of wine and riot, he stumbled blindly over
a wriggling bundle of rags in the middle of the street.
The trained right hand flashed to the sword at his belt,
but came away again as a trembling, curly-haired
youngster scrambled out of the rags and backed slowly
away as he rubbed the sleep from his eyes. Longinus
almost smiled.

"And who art thou, asleep in the gutter at dawn?"

"I—I am Rufus, from Cyrene."

Longinus knew Cyrene. He had put down a rebellion there. They were hard men to keep in line, the Cyrenians. Always revolting, for ever spilling blood. But this startled youngster looked like anything but a dealer in revolt.

"And why art thou here, Rufus of Cyrene?"

"For the Passover, with my father. He—he's lost me."

Longinus grunted, tugged at his sword again. Was he to be guardian to the lost children of Jerusalem, as well as executioner of Jerusalem's thieves? Let the brat find his father; it was none of his business, anyway: "Well, go find him then. And have a care where you go to-day. You may be hurt. Better get thee into a cellar and stay; yokels are out of place in a mob." And without so much as another glance he wheeled and went off down the street.

Now military heels have always played Pied Pipers' tunes to the hearts of little boys. Rufus knew that tune when he heard it. Enchanted, wondering what was meant by this talk of mobs and being hurt, the twelve-year-old followed until the man of war disappeared within the door of the city prison. Then he sat down to wait.

Other boys came, and men. As the crowd grew, a confusing gibberish found its way into the ears of the spellbound boy: "There are three of them: two thieves, and a crazy prophet from Galilee. . . . Barabbas got away again, the rascal. He'll start more trouble, you'll see. . . . He helped a lot of people, but Pilate was afraid. . . . The witnesses lied." It all meant nothing to Rufus except that three men were to die—and he, lucky boy, was to see them die.

Suddenly they came. The prison door flew open, like the black mouth of a great hungry animal, and a bedlam of shouts and curses came forth to meet the shouting of the mob. Two kicking, squirming, fear-maddened men, with huge beams of oak lashed across their shoulders, were dragged out into the sun. Behind them, quietly, came a third. His eyes were bloodshot, his body a mass of cuts and bruises. The soldiers did not push or curse this man: they seemed to pity, almost admire him, as they led him out and down the street.

There was Longinus, leading the procession, carrying a little white sign. People read it and shouted with laughter: "He's a king, is he? King of the Jews! No wonder the Romans are killing him." Rufus was nudged aside by a man who sneaked swiftly from one to another in the crowd, speaking softly: "Shout at him. Throw this stone at him. He is a blasphemer who would tear down the Synagogue. He has made trouble for the priests." Rufus didn't believe it. This man a king, with his arms bound to a wooden beam, going so quietly up to die? A blasphemer? He was not cursing, like the thieves.

A few stones were thrown as the column moved toward the city gate. A few of the bolder ones even reached out to strike the "king," only to be hurled back by the Romans. The quiet one did not see the stones, did not even seem to hear the angry shouts that greeted him. He was having trouble with his burden. He walked slower and slower, staggered a bit now and then. A hush went over the jeering mob as he fell, with a low moan, at the feet of white-faced Longinus. Quickly they unlaced the ropes, while the centurion scanned the crowd for a strong man to help the fallen one. His eye was halted by a massive pair of shoulders and a pair of arms that were like two great knots of iron. "Thou! Come here!" With a shout that was half a sob, young Rufus tore himself loose from the crowd and ran to the big fellow now in the clutch of the Romans. This was his father, Simon, and they were going to hurt him. Rufus clung to him, even kicked out at the shins of Longinus. Simon of Cyrene smiled courage and understanding into the lad, and threw him his cloak as he straddled the fallen beam and wrapped about it his bulging swarthy arms. The thieves were hustled to their feet, the soldiers got into line and the cruelest march of time was on again.

The rest was a bitter dream for Rufus. He heard the

ring of hammers and the screams of pain. The thieves were shouting and railing at the crowd, the quiet one was white with agony as the three black crosses went up against the sky. Rufus, sickened at a sight he had come to enjoy, went running from the hill, and collided with a shouting, drunken fellow who kicked him roughly aside. It was Barabbas, come with his old cronies to watch the fun. Barabbas was drunk, half with wine and half with unexpected freedom. He had fully expected to die where these fellows were dying, but a trick of fate had turned him loose. Hands on hips and legs astride, he stood before the center cross and looked up into the face of Jesus Christ. Something stronger than wine made him reel and almost fall. The leering grin flew from his face, his hands were trembling as he dashed them across his eyes: "Jehovah God! That's *my* cross he's dying on."

(What happened to you after Calvary, Barabbas? Were you highwayman and murderer again? And have you been hearing, in your haunted tomb, the echoing of that cry of yours in the throats of a hundred million men across the aisles of time: "That's *my* cross he died upon"?)

What had he done, this Barabbas-substitute? Nothing, except to break through the isolating, narrowing little fences of the Pharisees and the Governors. Nothing, except to make of the world one parish, to bind together all peoples as subjects of one great Ruler, mightier than Cæsar. Nothing, that is, except to be different. But to be different is to be dangerous—and damned. This Jesus was dangerous to the unchanging, unsatisfying religion of old Israel. He had upset the conventional sanctions of the Law, preached new and damaging doctrine, put the picture of God in a new frame. He had declared that God was a Father who ruled through love and not by vested authority, that religion was of the heart and not of the statute books. He had led crowds out of the synagogues, where worship had become blasphemy because it was performed by men with unclean hearts, and he had taught them to find this loving God in the lilies of the field, in salt and mustard seed and prodigals and Magdalenes.

He was dangerous to the old morality, the old ethics. Genuine righteousness, he said, came out of a new relation to God, not through blind obedience to the written laws of men. He sought to make clean the motives of men, and let actions take care of themselves. Man might defy the old Law and pluck wheat on the Sabbath, or draw an ox from a well or heal the sick, as long as he worshiped God with all his heart and mind and strength and loved his neighbor as himself. A man must always do unto others as he wanted others to do unto him. Fallen women were to be helped, not stoned. Jews were to love Samaritans.

He was dangerous to Pilate, to Cæsar, to the State. He talked of the tearing down of cities and of the building of another kingdom which Cæsar, dull-witted and national, could never understand. He wanted to divide the allegiance of men between God and Cæsar, and he talked of peace and forgiveness and the turning of the other cheek in a day of thundering legions and blood and the short-sword. He was impossible, idealistic, revolutionary. He died because he wanted to make over the heart of a smug and satisfied world which was continually to resist the march of his spirit. He convinced only Eleven Men of the truth and power of his gospel, of his chances of overcoming the world. He taught them well, showed them by his own living that it might be done, and he left them saying: "Ye are the salt of the earth . . . ye are the light of the world."

But the light of the world nearly flickered out that first Good Friday night. Those Eleven Men ran like frightened sheep, crawled off into eleven shadows to hide from the pointing fingers of Jerusalem. Only one of them braved the light of day—John the Beloved went with the two Marys to the scene of the cross. One other died that night—Judas swung, a suicide, from the limb of another tree.

At the ninth hour Jesus died, and two pilgrims of the night came to claim his body. Nicodemus, the half-convinced, and Arimathean Joseph, converts from the very Sanhedrin that condemned him, took him down as the sky went crimson overhead and the earth rocked beneath their feet. Longinus, still in command, sealed the tomb with Cæsar's seal, looked over his shoulder as he worked, at the three bleak crosses on the hill. "Well, it's over. I will report to Pilate and Caiaphas that it is done, that he is dead, that he will trouble us no more. But—I wonder."

Next day it was quiet in Jerusalem, and under the spell of that quietness, the Eleven crept forth from their shadows, and went running to one another. Simon Peter, James and John, Andrew, Matthew—what do they have to say now? Wonder has given way to doubt and sick discouragement in their hearts. Philip, Bartholomew, and Thomas the Doubter; James of Alpheus, Judas Thaddeus and Simon the Canaanite—they are all prisoners to hopelessness. The whole lot of them are beaten and cowed. The salt is losing its savor, trust and courage have gone out of them. The Rock, the Doubter and the Sons of Zebedee return to ride the tides of Galilee again. Back to humdrum, after this touch of the life abundant. Back——

But it was not to be. Men are to be stopped in the streets of Jerusalem and stare incredulous as they heard: "He has risen from the tomb!" Annas and Caiaphas are to toss for many a sleepless night as the thought pounds

in their brains: "He has conquered us—and death."
Peter is to leap from his foolish little fisher-boat as it
dawns upon him that this Jesus can not die. The Eleven
come boldly now, back to the city, laughing at Roman
spears and the mutterings of the Pharisees, possessed of
the strength of mad men. "He is alive. He is here."
Across all Jerusalem, in every poor man's hovel and rich
man's palace, it is heard. It flies out along the blue Ti-
berian lake, up and down the byways of Judea, down the
road to Athens and to Rome. "Jesus Christ is alive.
He can not die. He is come back to rule the hearts of
men." However you may explain, wise scholars; or
analyze, psychologists; however you may quarrel over it,
historian; or sneer, laugh or only smile, you common
man, it was this and nothing else that built the Christian
Church and that saved the Christian spirit and ethic for
all of us. Belief in the risen Christ, in the abiding presence of their Lord, drew that band together again and
made them over from cowards into eleven of the greatest benefactors of the human race. Their faith made
of Jesus Christ the most tremendous fact in human
history and of his teaching and spirit the greatest single
factor that has ever turned tides in the affairs of men.
Back they come, eleven remade men, to march with
this spirit for ever and a day, into countless millions of
battles for the truth of God. Back they come and out
they go, Eleven Men against the world with nothing in

their hands but staffs and no weapons but the love of Christ.

The march of Eleven Men!

Among their first recruits were a firebrand named Stephen and a fanatic named Saul.

CHAPTER II

THE FIRST MILE

STEPHEN was deacon as well as firebrand, and that fact is interesting. It gives a hint of the manner in which the early Church went at the world. Deacons were especially charged with "the care of the poor," something new in religion. Philanthropy, in the new faith, becomes religious duty; worshipers are encouraged to share their property and wealth, communist-like, that all may have an equal share, an equal opportunity. The lot of the poor, in these very first days, is made less difficult, less hopeless; not only emancipated slaves but emancipated paupers as well come out of these early records like ghost-ships out of the night. The common man, the less-than-average man, got his first real chance as Christianity dug into his world; and his chances of better life rose and fell as the spirit of Christ in the hearts of men rose and fell. Later ages were to prove that at times when their chances seemed gone for ever, when injustice and inequality were to rule again, that some son of Deacon Stephen would rise and champion them. There was the gentle Saint Francis of Assisi, poorest man that ever lived, who left the world so rich; there was

Wesley preaching to his dirty-faced miners at Gwennap Pit; there was General Booth and his big bass drum.

Perhaps this Deacon Stephen should have been satisfied with the administration of charity-money. He wasn't. The spell was upon him to preach. And he preached not wisely but too well; he had more fervor than caution. He never preached a soft or merely "comforting" sermon; his words were like burning spears of fire. He preached everywhere and to every one. The gutters of Jerusalem were his pulpit, the cosmopolitan crowds of the market-place, drawn from the ends of the earth, his congregation. He stirred them and won their sympathy. He stirred the Sanhedrin—not to sympathy but to rage. Incensed at the brutal frankness of his oratory, they haled him into court, they questioned him, warned, threatened and cajoled. But who can "warn" truth, or threaten it? Firebrand Stephen blazed back at them: "Ye stiff-necked and uncircumcised . . . ye have been now . . . betrayers and murderers." It was too much, too brazen, too dangerous to the tottering authority of this clan of ruling Jews. (And shall we keep it in mind that Jewry at large did not kill Christ or Stephen? They might have accepted both had it not been for the stupid tactics of these frightened, intolerant leaders.) They pounced upon him, thrust him out into an open space and stoned him to death.

The war was on! Freedom and conscience are to be

the stakes in an everlasting battle with force, intolerance, political stupidity and greed. The self-appointed
executioners curse and hurl their stones, thinking they
might bury with them not only Stephen but his God
and Christ as well. Little did they know that they were
laying the foundation of a mightier Church than mankind had ever known before: that out of their stones
were to grow hospitals, orphanages, houses of refuge,
Peace-Palaces-At-The-Hague and cathedrals Notre
Dame and York. Little did they know that on the edge
of that ring of death about Stephen there stood a man
who was to be the layer of the corner-stone!

The murderers, working beneath a blazing sun,
stripped off their cloaks to give their savage arms free
play, and threw them into the arms of a young Jew on
the edge of the crowd. Saul, a native of Tarsus, was a
graduate of the theological school of the Jerusalem
Pharisees, filled with fanatical zeal for the law of Moses
and burning with hatred for the sect of the Nazarene.
He "made havoc of the church, entering into every
house, and haling men and women, committed them to
prison." Dealer in fire and death, he worked well until
he was held up in his course at a blazing turn on the
Damascus Road. What happened there we have no
time to debate. All we know is that Saul the Persecutor
met the Christ he hated; that the persecutor within him
died and that Paul the Christian was born. He heard a

voice and he answered it; his life was turned as a boulder turns the current of a stream. Saul, now become Paul, falls in step with the Eleven, outstrips them, becomes the greatest missionary star that ever shot up into the sky of Christian history. He made Jesus international when the Jews would have kept him national and weak. He won the allegiance of cultured Greece, put into men's hearts a more powerful law than Rome's, and began to rear a new world upon the ruins of the old.

Paul was three men rolled into one. He was Jew by birth, Roman by citizenship, Greek by culture and study. He moved all his days in a world ruled by the Roman, taught and made beautiful by the Greek (history calls it the Greco-Roman world), and filled with scattered and wandering Jews. He spent his life influenced by and influencing these three races. He began with the Jews, and he had a hard time of it.

Any man has a hard time of it when he tries to reform an institution from within, especially when it is a religious institution. Religious ideas and customs harden, like arteries; they are the last of all ideas to change. It was true in the day of Martin Luther and of Wesley, and it was true in the day of Paul. The Jews did not want this new God of Paul; they were afraid, timid, slow to let go of the old. The old gods are always good enough; the old ways always best. They did not hesitate to tell him so, and he was anything but popular with his kinsmen. They did their best to get rid of him as he traveled up and down the coasts of Asia Minor: they hounded him from town to town, from jail to jail. "Of the Jews," he says, "five times received I forty stripes save one. Thrice was I beaten with rods, once was I stoned, thrice I suffered shipwreck, a night and a day have I been in the deep." A prophet has no honor—in his own country.

He did his best for them, won a few of them, gave them Christian churches, but they turned him out— they would have none of him. He received kindlier treatment from the Greeks in Asia Minor than he did from the Jews. As a missionary to his own he was a failure. And he might have died as one of the Great Unknown had he not the heart of a Crusader, the call of far places in his blood. He stood one day on the shore of the Hellespont, and looked across at Europe. Over there in the fogs of the other bank was Greece! Philippi, Corinth, above all Athens. It was inevitable that Paul should cross the Hellespont, that he should come to grips with the learning of Greece in its own haunts, for he had been influenced by it in numerous ways. He knew the philosophy and art of the Greeks; he respected the scholarship of Greece and he was drawn to it as fine steel is drawn by a magnet, with a keen desire to use it for his Christ. So we find him, one fine day, disappearing across the horizon into Macedonia, the homeland of Alexander the Great, that riotous young genius who whipped the earth to his feet and died at thirty years of age.

Paul moved all his life in the shadow of this mighty Alexander of Macedon. Indeed, the whole world lived in his shadow. He had conquered every land and people within reach, and spread everywhere the civilization of classic Greece. He forced this conquered world to think in Greek, talk, live and die in Greek. He was possessed of an amazing dream: to give the world one language (Greek) ; to make of all men one race and blood (noble-men, gentlemen, like the Greeks); to give them one culture, one ruler, and one God. He took ten thousand Macedonian soldiers and married them off to ten thousand maidens from Persia and India. He tried to make the world one nation, one individual, one kind; he tried to give them everything—and failed. It never occurred to Alexander that men, to be one, must have in their hearts the same spirit, as well as the same features on their faces. Paul saw that, and he trailed the shadow of the military genius through the Greek-saturated world, giving what Alexander failed to give: the fourth dimension of the spirit.

We say Paul did it; we should say Paul plus. For there went out on the roads of that Greco-Roman world a nameless host who will never be honored as we honor Paul and the Eleven Men who walked with Jesus Christ.

There were a thousand unknown soldiers of the Cross, during these first three hundred years, who preached and struggled and died, leaving behind them a finer world than they marched into. Some of them we know. Our Eleven leave us now in physical form, to lead the march in spirit so long as time shall last. James the brother of Jesus and James the son of Zebedee preach and are killed by mobs in Jerusalem; Matthew is slain on a sword in Ethiopia; Philip is hanged in Phrygia; Bartholomew flayed alive in Armenia. Andrew is crucified in Achaia, Thomas is run through with a lance in East India, Thaddeus is shot to death with arrows, a cross goes up in Persia for Simon the Zealot, and another in Rome for Peter. Matthias is beheaded; only John escaped a martyr's grave. A fair record, is it not, for eleven "weaklings," who once ran to hide? All over the then known world they sent up their myriad of steeples to the sky, they left a Church for Christ in every nook and corner of the earth. By the beginning of the fourth century a writer tells us: "There is not a single race of human beings, barbarians, Greeks or whatever name you please to call them, nomads or vagrants or herdsmen living in tents, where prayers in the name of Jesus the Crucified are not offered up." A broad statement, full of holes, perhaps. But this much is certain: the new faith not only had a foothold in this world of Roman law and Grecian culture, but it was uprooting

old religions, undermining an old and decadent morality,
building a new ethic based neither on military might nor
esthetics but on love. It was making over, putting new
heart into an exhausted, outworn, disillusioned and disheartened civilization.

There was Athens, for instance. Is there any stranger
sight in all of history than the spectacle of the Apostle
Paul, outcast Pharisee and renegade Jew, walking up the
streets in Athens? An unknown, fantastic prophet of a
"crazy" faith which claimed that its founder had risen
from the dead! He was coming to tell Athens *that!*
How ridiculous of you, Paul: no one could tell a Greek
anything. Had not they been telling the world all
things, themselves, for centuries? Had not Socrates been
here, Plato and Aristotle? Had not Phidias carved his
Parthenon, and Homer, blind father of song, given the
world *The Iliad?* Had there not been the Golden Age
in Greece, which some still call the greatest age of man?

That was just the trouble. Socrates *had* been there; the
Golden Age *had* been. It was behind them, gone for
ever when Paul of Tarsus came to Athens. He entered
a city and met a culture which were not even poor imi-
tations of "the glory which was Greece," but which
were sick and ready to die. All their fine philosophies,
built upon the emphasis on the individual, had failed to
produce an enviable individual. They were disgusting,
even as pagans. They had lost their sense of balance and

their nerve. They were afraid to go on living in a universe in which they could not find a sympathetic God.
Socrates, for all his wisdom, proved better at asking
questions than at answering them: he had led the Greeks
up a blind alley of despair, to a final blank wall of
ignorance.

The Stoics, flower of their reasoning and in full bloom
when Jesus died and Paul began, could offer no way out.
Listen to the encouragement offered by Marcus Aurelius,
one of their greatest sons: "He who is forty years old . . .
has seen all things which have been and all that will be."
They had nothing to live for; suicides in Athens were so
numerous that they became alarming.

They had a hundred gods, revered not one of them,
and became cynical about all of them. Common men
rebuked these gods for not keeping their promises, for
indulging in indecencies which they could not tolerate
among themselves. Zeus, Aphrodite, Mars, Hermes and
the rest had lost their effectiveness in a deluge of disgusting practises. The Greeks were hard put to it for
a God: they went chasing after magicians, impostors,
prognosticators and quacks. They no longer even con-
sulted the tripod at the Acropolis. They put their trust
in chewing laurel leaves, in spitting to ward off evil
omens. Philosophically, they were run down; spiritually, they were bankrupt.

Their morality, too, had given out. Veniality, sexual

license and brutality widened and became the order of
the day. Slavery ate into their strength like a fatal
cancer; even Aristotle could defend it. The greatest
inequality that men have ever known was this Greek
inequality with an aristocracy of brains at one end and
the slave, often worth less than an animal, at the other.
Prostitution was wide-spread and approved, corruption
and thievery and public scandal ran riot through society
and government. Democracy was a trembling, fading
hope. They may have had a "thought-out" world, as
some scholars claim. But they also had a world that was
tired out, and waiting for the crack of doom. Instead
of destruction came Christianity, bearing deliverance.
Paul, pilgrim of the long road, walked into their midst
and while they stared incredulous, he went up Mars Hill,
stood in the very shadow of their awesome Parthenon,
and preached on "The Unknown God."

Like the lad who thrust his finger into the hole in the
dike, the Apostle came at precisely the right moment to
hold back the flood. He did not bring back the old
glory to Greece, nor the old power to Rome. It is
hard to save a man or a nation that is three-quarters
dead. The new faith came too late to save much of the
old order of things. But Paul and the Christ of Paul
did build in that crumbling, rotten society a new kind
of man: the very man the Greeks had dreamed about.
They conquered fear in that man by putting love at the

center of his universe. They relegated myth and superstition and magic and Emperor-worship to the limbo of
forgotten things, and put in their places an ennobling
worship of one God who was personal, righteous and
powerful. They gave a sense of freshness to a world
gone stale, a ray of hope to a world in distress. Where
death and despair had nearly conquered, there came a
ringing shout, "I am come that men might have life, and
have it more abundantly!"

That cry reached everybody, but it reached first the
common man. The wise men tried to laugh him out
of town: they scorned his discourse on Mars Hill as so
much gibberish. That laughter hurt. He went,
chagrined, to other labors and tried to forget the wise
Athenians. He never forgot them: he was sensitive
about his failure until the day he died. But he had not
failed. The common man listened to him as he had
listened to Jesus—gladly. And why not? If you had
been a slave in Athens, would you not have listened to
talk of freedom, equality and justice? Paul encouraged
the slave and the under-dog to dare to hope again. They
dared; they talked about it to every one. They organized
in little groups and societies. Slave girls whispered the
good news into the ears of their rich mistresses, and
patrician owners of huge numbers of slaves began to
ask them questions. Of course, they laughed at the an-
swers they got. But the laughter died as they began

to see a better type of character than their philosophies had been able to produce. Slaves, under-dogs, men of the "lower classes" were showing themselves to be finer men than their masters. Men *were* different under this new way of life; character *was* being changed; Christians *were* a finer type. The one thing, above all else, that made Christianity a conqueror in old Greece was the proof of power in the changed lives of its adherents. They "out-thought, out-lived, out-died their contemporaries!" They began to say to the philosophers: "We do not speak great things. We live them!"

Have you heard the tale that there was no real conquest of the Greek mind by Jesus? That it was only "a religion of slaves"? Every generation has heard that from the cynical. The accusation is not true, but even if it were, what of it? Is it to be held against Christianity that it started with fishermen and tax-collectors and ended with emperors and kings? Is it to be considered failure that it reached first the people who needed it most, the sick who were in greatest need of a physician? We have read a thousand pages brimming over with tears and sentimentalism about the noble beautiful death of Socrates: a truly noble and heroic death. But there remains another story to be written: the story of the miracle of character-changing which induced slaves and under-dogs and ex-cowards to die like Socrates!

History is an eloquent denial of this weak charge that Christianity for old Greece was only a religion of the lower classes. The truth of the matter is that it squared itself with and entirely won the respect and devotion of the finest, keenest minds and deepest scholarship of that intellectual center of the earth. "Paul reborn in Christ," says Gilbert Murray, "is certainly one of the great figures of Greek literature."

Read what Greeks wrote after Paul had left Mars Hill, and see that Christ has won out over Socrates. Justin Martyr, ex-Stoic and ex-pagan and a leading philosopher of Greece, wrote: "Christianity is the oldest, truest, most divine of all philosophies." He wrote that, and in support of that verdict he died a martyr's death. Clement of Alexandria declared that Greek philosophy is fulfilled in Christianity. Origen, boldest thinker of them all; Athanasius; the two Gregories and Chrysostom the "golden-mouthed": Christ took every one of them. Truly the Eleven Men had swept the scholarship of the most impregnable citadels of ancient learning to the foot of the cross of the Nazarene, and made it worship there. Christianity took prisoner the finest learning of Athens, Alexandria and Antioch. A "religion of slaves," forsooth!

Paul had one more road to travel. There was one stronghold that seemed impossible for him to take: it was the City of the Seven Hills. Greece supplied the

world with learning and with art, but Rome held it
tight in her great mailed fist. She conquered it and
governed it, and she forced on every one the bitter
truth that all roads led to Rome. As Paul comes down
to Rome, he hears the roar of the crowd at the Circus;
Christians are staining the sand with the crimson red
of their blood, while brutal arrogant Rome looks on and
laughs. Nero, fat and going crazy, sits in his royal box
watching a handful of ludicrous Christians struggle
with the mightiest Empire beneath the sun. What will
Rome do to you, you aging Saul of Tarsus? And what
will you do to Rome?

CHAPTER III

ROME

ROME. ROME. *ROME!* Eternal City, set on seven
hills. City of grandeur and terror and pitiful collapse.
City that chained the world, then died at the other
end of the chain. Rome! No schoolboy to-day can
pronounce that name without a quicker running of his
blood. And no man, woman or child in that first
century after Christ could hear of it or even think of
it without a thrill of pride or a look of startled fear.

Rome was a tyrant: she stood with her foot on the
neck of the world. Carthage dared to oppose her, and
was wiped out, burned and torn down to the level of
the earth. Romans were known the world around as
ambassadors of the terrible short-sword; they hacked
and stabbed their way to victory over every city they
could find: they took every people, chained, to serve as
slaves.

Rome was road-builder to the world. Who has not
heard of the Appian Way? Wherever her thundering
legions went, went those everlasting Roman roads. Go
to England or France to-day and see them: you will
never believe that they were built by crude hand-

labor, with steam-shovels and cement undreamed of.
Rome was architect and builder. Remarkable
aqueducts carried rivers of water down from the hills
to her two million inhabitants. Giant sewers, roofed
with hewn stone, large enough to send a street-car
through, formed a labyrinth beneath her streets.
Houses were piped with running water, filled with
works of art, echoed with the splashing of water-
fountains in the courtyard. There were three theaters
in Rome, an amphitheater and a hundred temples; there
was the Forum, the Capitol, the palaces of the Cæsars.

Rome was also the play-boy of the ancient world.
Her multitudes were enlivened by endless chariot races,
gladiatorial combats and public banquets. Crassus,
Roman triumvir, who was alive when Paul came to
Rome, gave one-tenth of his millions to the people, as
a man throws pennies to a mob of fighting boys; he held
a banquet of ten thousand tables, and fed the whole
city for three long months. Cæsar, in the year 65, gave
a gladiatorial show in which three hundred pairs of
slave gladiators fought to the death. When the mobs
tired of slaves, wild beasts were brought in: elephants,
tigers, crocodiles and lions faced the gladiatorial sword
while the real beast, the Roman mob, went shouting
mad for the sight of blood. One show followed another
so quickly that every day soon became show-day, every
spectacle more gorgeous, cruel and bloody than the last.

Whatever else may be said of her, Rome was a bene-factor of priceless gifts to men. She bound that old world together with her splendid highways, eliminating time and space in faster transportation, drawing the world into a narrower circle. She gave the world a priceless code of law and developed what has been called the "law of races." Echoes of that gift are found in 1932, in the law-codes of Europe and America. It was harsh law, cruel law, at times, but if a conquered people learned to accept it and live within it, peace and pros-perity came to them. Rome made the world a safer place to live in, cleared the seas of pirates, the roads of highwaymen. Stable government was another of her gifts. Strong, centralized and efficient, that government ruled over a vaster area of land and held together a greater number of men and tongues than had ever been ruled and held by any other nation. In these respects Rome was superb. Yet beneath the glitter and grandeur there was developing a fatal yellow streak, aye, streaks of rust that were a prelude to decay were come into their iron souls to turn them from thundering conquerors to weak and flabby fools. The ruler and the conqueror was in the throes of death. His place was being taken by a lesser Roman who only wanted to loaf in the sun, to drink good wines, to loll in luxury while the rest of the world writhed in chains. This shouting Roman at the amphitheater had forgotten how to work and how to fight. He lived on the labor of a multitude of slaves, and in constant fear of a slave rebellion. That was inevitable. When the freemen of Rome numbered three hundred and twenty thousand, their slaves were nine hundred thousand. But at the beginning of the Empire, 27 B.C., there were a million and a half in chains in Italy alone. The once-glorious legions thundered less and less until finally they thundered not at all. The old and stirring battle-cries were drowned out of memory by the cowardly screaming of the crowd for the blood of the gladiator. "The People," wrote Campanella, Italian philosopher, "the people is a beast of muddy brain."

So when the Eleven marched into Rome they faced— that. In Athens they had fought and won the scholarship of the old world; they had faced nothing worse than sarcasm and bitter laughter and the opposition of the mind. But in Rome they faced deliberate physical cruelty, fiendish persecution at the hands of a degenerate race of men gone soft with sex license, luxury and laziness, led by a degenerate Nero. These were the enemies who lay in wait for the coming legions of the Lord: a people morally gone to pieces and complacent about it, a rival religion or set of religions based upon incredible myths and on a ritual which was morally repulsive and shot through with a formalism that had not the least relation to life and the morals of life; a

State that thought of men only as soldier-fodder or as human bricks for the foundations of Empire, and a monster of an Emperor who, with his successors and predecessors, snuffed out the life of any subject who refused to worship him, who would not honor him before the gods—or God.

Truly, there was no shortage of gods in Rome. It was easier to find a god there than to find a man. The gods of all the earth had been brought back, with the human captives, from the foreign wars. Zeus, Minerva, Dionysos, Apollo and Diana had come from Greece; Isis and Osiris from Egypt; Mithra from Persia. One new god, more or less, would not have meant much in Rome. If Christianity's God had been as harmless as all the rest of them, there would never have been any trouble. Rome was always tolerant of religions and gods until they interfered with Rome. The Christians got into trouble in refusing to worship the Emperor, in mixing politics with religion, and in holding their meetings in secret.

The old gods were myths, and their worshipers knew it. So did the Christians, who realized that to win over their rivals they had to supply with their God something the old ones had not given. They did it: Christianity began with nothing more impressive than a company of despised slaves, but it won out because it was a better religion than any other at the Capital. These

slaves conquered the paganism of their masters and became salt in the wounds of a sorry world. They offered
men a new freedom in a new heaven and made their
present world a better place to live in. Against the
teaching of brutish Roman military might came the
teaching that love was a better weapon than the short-
sword, a teaching clinched and proved by the behavior
of the Christians. Over against the banquet-orgies and
the squandering of wealth came the idea of the sharing
and responsibility of wealth—the dawn of Christian
charity. That stung like salt and fire in the sodden
minds of those Romans who had become accustomed to
scrambling for the favors of the rich, and who wanted
the squandering and the lavishing to go on. Against
the waste of Roman life and energy came the theory
of the equality of all mankind, of the ultimate value
and purpose of human personality.

There were softer messages these Christians might
have preached, less dangerous doctrines which would
have kept them out of trouble and prevented persecution. There were easier, less hazardous fields to which
they might have gone. But the march of the Eleven
Men has never become a retreat: the spirit of Christ in
the hearts of men has never turned to run from the
hard task. It has always seized upon those tasks which
seemed impossible. Let the cynical remember that it
set its face at the very outset against political tyranny,

that it began to fight slavery in a day when the rulers
of earth lived on the labor of slaves, and that it fought
slavery to the end. This spirit has faced economic
greed, beaten it down, released women and children
from the factory and the mines, and made labor a thing
of dignity, even when Christians were shouting:
"Laissez-faire," which means, in substance, "Mind your
own business; keep your hands off." And remember
particularly that in these days of the collapse of the
Roman Empire and in the subsequent "Dark" Ages, the
progress achieved was measured in terms of the progress of Christianity. The Eleven have never retreated!

The first onslaught in Rome was terrible, enough to
halt any movement or break up any institution that
did not have within it the seeds of truth and eternal
life. Nero, legend says, set fire to Rome and played
his silly violin while Rome burned. That may or may
not be true, but true it certainly is that his reign was a
mad melody of stupid persecution, the last discords of
which were drowned out in a shout of rage as Rome,
aroused, shook its fist in his face. Startled and frightened, Nero pointed his finger at the already unpopular
Christians and cried: "They did it." That was enough:
fickle Rome rushed off to the amphitheater to see them
die. Nero outdid himself; he covered the Christians
with pitch, burned them as torches in his gardens. He
clothed them in the hides of animals, sent them into the

arena against tigers and lions and wild boars. He set
his gladiators upon them, he fed them in droves to the
beasts. He and his mob, blind and stupid, could not
see what was happening beneath their very eyes: that
this rabble of Christians was coming to grips in the
sand of the Circus with the rotten spirit and ethics of
a Rome that deserved to die and was priming herself
for death. They could not know that thrashing about
in the bloody sand were the ghosts of Eleven Men,
helping these new recruits to die, to strangle this Roman
Empire to death, to build amid the wreckage a new
world in which the cruelty of the amphitheater would
be impossible.

It began right there: in the sand, in a fight against the
spirit of the gladiatorial combat and the lust to see men
die. That was, perhaps, the hardest place on earth to
begin, for nothing was more deeply imbedded in Roman
nature than this love of cruel sport. Even chariot
races were tame for them unless some driver went down
beneath the wheels. Foot races? Discus throwing?
That was tame; let the weak Greeks go in for that.
Rome thrilled and cheered when Emperor Trajan thrust
ten thousand pairs of gladiators into the arena to fight
for their lives in a holiday one hundred and twenty-
three days long. They cheered even louder when
Domitian sent women out to fight and die. Symmachus,
a prefect, planned a birthday party for his little son

in which a large troop of Saxon prisoners were to fight
one another. The Saxons disappointed the little fellow
by strangling each other to death the night before the
show. Symmachus was inconsolable with chagrin, but
it turned to rage when a Christian said to him: "No one
should perish in the city whose punishment is an amusement." That was a new note in the sporting world!

Even the Christians were attracted to these shows.
One convert, says Augustine, sneaked in to watch a
spectacle, but sat, guiltily, with his hands over his eyes.
His uncovered ears betrayed him: the shouts of the
crowd reached into his heart, and soon he was cheering
with the best of them. But *this man was made an outcast from the Church.* And that may reveal something
of the secret of the power of the early Church: any
man was liable to be put out of it at any time.

It was a long hard fight against the roots of cruelty in
human nature. As late as 400 A.D. Christians were rep-
rimanded for attending the games. The victory did
not come at once, not overnight, not in a hundred years.
But the fact remains that Christianity, with a feeble
allay in Stoicism, tore this love of cruel sport, root and
branch, out of Roman life and custom. The fact remains that these sports were at their height when Paul
came over the first of the seven hills, and that until
that coming, Isis and Osiris and all the rest of the old
battalion of gods in Rome had proved powerless against

them: they had not even tried to correct the evil. But the influence of the new gospel was felt at once, and it continued until that bright red-letter day when a Christian monk named Telemachus leaped out of a box at the amphitheater and demanded, at the price of his life, that the cruel business stop. That was the end of the gladiatorial combats and bloody shows. Telemachus left his body in the sand with those of the victims he leaped in to help—but he won. He has found an earthly immortality in one great unwritten law of Christian civilization, that bloody sport and cruel amusement are never to return.

The fight is still on, but it is not so desperate. It is a far cry, for instance, from Rome in the fifth century to Newark, New Jersey, in the twentieth. An editorial protest appeared in the *Newark Evening News* in November of 1930, when a matador (from Brooklyn) sought to put on a Spanish bull-fight at a Newark amusement park: "A real bull-fight would be intolerable, and a burlesque, such as now has been suggested, would be an imposition on an audience. It ought to fail of its own grotesqueness." Professor Phelps, of Yale, protesting to Newark's Mayor, felt that "However harmlessly the thing is handled, there is danger that it might degenerate into cruelty." A veritable army of the sons of Telemachus may be found in the ranks of organizations like the S.P.C.A., or the S.P.C.C., whose everlasting battle is against the inhumanity of man to beast and man to child. A Wild-West show in Madison Square Garden was nearly disrupted by a protest against the roping of calves and the bull-dogging of steers. You believe in sport-without-bloodshed, do you, Modern Man? You want clean wholesome athletics? You will howl down, instinctively, foul or cruel tactics in any sport? Where did you get that instinct? You picked it up out of the sand of the amphitheater at Rome, and you have been enlarging on it across twenty centuries of Christian development.

Nero died. Other monsters came. Decius, "the accursed wild beast," filled the jails with singing Christians. Valerian, the heartless, and Diocletian, the unspeakable, added horror to horror. Even Marcus Aurelius, whose beautiful *Meditations* is still accepted as the prayer-book of paganism, sanctioned the burning of Polycarp, Bishop of Smyrna, a tottering old man of eighty-six years; he also caused to be beheaded Justin Martyr, who lived better than a Stoic and died like a god. Indeed, the technique of death possessed by the Christians won for them the very sympathy that the Emperors had hoped to crush. There was a new appeal in it, never heard before by Roman ears. The old Romans died for the Empire, like blind and faithful dogs. But these Christians died like Jesus Christ, with their eyes wide open to what was happening. They reached out their arms in the form of the Cross—to touch the outstretched hands of the eleven ghost-marchers in the skies.

In the wake of the monsters and the persecutors came Constantine, the first Christian Emperor and the most debated man in history. He inherited from the old Emperors a little of the brute. It was rumored that he was the murderer of his wife, his father-in-law and his own son. He has been called the benefactor and the enemy of the Church. Probably he was both. He was benefactor in that his laws ended the persecutions of the Christians. He gave them not only tolerance, but protection and encouragement. He swept from their bloody shoulders the sackcloth and ashes of poverty and put there instead the royal purple of the State. He gave them power, which they have often abused; respectability, which is sometimes an enemy of real love and charity. But despite these lapses we see the influence of the Christian teachings in the laws of Constantine and his followers more clearly than ever before. We are interested not so much in what Constantine was as we are in what through him happened to the world in which he lived. A great deal happened.

Chapter IV

IN HOC SIGNO VINCES

CONSTANTINE was the son of a brilliant general, Constantius the Sallow, and of a village barmaid. In his climb to power he used the methods of both. He soon learned to make shrewd use of everything that came his way: even of that famous vision in the sky. In his war with Maxentius, we are told, he saw the vision of a cross suspended in the clouds, and beneath it, in letters of fire, were the words, *In Hoc Signo Vinces*. We of to-day no longer look for signs in the heavens, but we still write those words on our church windows, telling our children that they mean, "By this sign we conquer." Constantine certainly conquered. He pushed Maxentius into the Tiber and drowned him with a thousand of his men; he displaced the historic Roman eagle on the flag-poles of Rome and put there the Cross of Christ. He ended the influence of paganism in Roman law and substituted for it the nobler guiding spirit of Christianity. Even though the personal Christianity of Constantine may have been nothing better than a convention, the Christian spirit which stayed behind him in his laws, and which came to dominate the legislation of his successors, is a real and vital thing. The face of Christ appears everywhere in the law that had once been harsh and cruel. In the glow of that countenance laws are made less and less often in the selfish interest of the rich and powerful, and they begin to consider the rights of the weak, of the women and the children and the slaves.

The first blow was struck at the very center of Roman injustice and cruelty: the tyranny of parental power in the home. It is hard for a modern father, who takes not only advice but often instruction as well from his modern wife and super-modern child, to appreciate the far-reaching and oppressive power in the hands of the Roman *paterfamilias.* That ancient father could chastise, put in chains, exile, sell as a slave or even murder his own child with the full protection of the law. He controlled every penny of his children's property, picked out wives for his sons and husbands for his daughters, separated them at will if he found them "temperamental." The Roman son, legally, was worse off than the Roman slave. Manlius put his own son to death for disobeying orders, and Cassius Brutus played executioner to his boy for communicating with the enemy. Children were dragged through the streets to the whipping post by their irate fathers, while groups of Roman "gentlemen" looked on with hearts of marble. Paul, a Stoical jurist, tells us that a father in Rome was quite justified in selling his son for cash in times of great need or poverty. That was the best the vaunted Roman law could do in the matter of relationships between father and son!

This was changed by Constantine, the new Emperor. One law issued in 333 A.D. threatened to punish as a parricide any father who takes the life of his son! Justinian, who came later, went even further. He allowed a father to inflict only minor penalties on his son, and required that more severe punishments be administered only after trial before a court! Constantine's law gave the son control over certain portions of his property: Justinian gave him full control over all his possessions. In the years between and after these two men, Christianity so saturated the laws that fathers were forbidden to buy or sell their sons; they could not imprison them without due trial, or send them to live in another home without their consent. Best of all, sons were allowed to choose their own wives, without the "advice and consent" of the father. Parental tyranny was done when the Christian spirit controlled the lawbooks of Rome. The laws made by the Christian Emperors who followed Constantine converted the rights of the Roman father into what are essentially the rights of the father of to-day. The power of the father under the old Roman law and under the laws of the Christian Emperors marks the difference between the old world and the new. Parental tyranny was doomed when the

child came to be recognized as the child of God as well
as of his earthly father, as "joint heir with Christ," equal
to the father in the eyes of God. That tyranny has
passed wherever the Eleven have marched. It may still
survive in an African jungle or in lost tribes in forgotten
corners of the earth, but in Christian Europe and
America we no longer chain our sons nor sell them for
cash. We study child psychology, and take our children
for walks in the park or countryside on Sunday afternoon.

Sunday afternoon! That is another thing Constantine
did for us, with the Eleven urging him from behind.
Sunday, before the Emperor saw his Cross in the clouds,
was merely another day. It meant no change of pace,
no difference of scene and action from the other six
days of the week. Soon after his coming to the throne
there appeared the first of a long line of "Sunday laws,"
designed in the interest of the working man. All labor,
other than that of men in the fields, was forbidden; all
civil servants were to have the day off, and all soldiers.
Slaves were granted this as a day of rest, and when we
realize the grueling, killing pace at which they were
driven, we appreciate the relief this one law must have
brought them. The gift of Sunday is one of the greatest external gifts of Christianity to the working classes:
it has relaxed the muscles of toil, restored the worker to
his family, and given him something else to think of

than mere gain. A law of Emperor Leo says: "On the Lord's Day, let no legal act be done; let no debtor receive a summons, let no pleadings be made, let there be no process, let the hard voice of the public crier be silent. . . ." Millions of people to-day escape the hard voices of the struggle for bread on that same Sunday holiday; it is the unusual, the undesirable job, that now forces a man to work seven days a week. But not one in a million ever stops to thank Constantine for that avenue of escape: Constantine, first Christian Emperor of Byzantium and Rome.

There was another member of the Roman family who was grateful for the coming of that day of rest, and the checking of the power of the father. That was the Roman woman. If it is hard for the modern father to understand the position of the ancient one, it is next to impossible for the modern mother to understand the position of the mother and woman of old Rome. Modern mother bobs her hair, votes for president, goes out and gets herself a job, does pretty much as she pleases with her time, her money and her children. A Roman mother would have been struck dead for even dreaming of such things. Far from being honored or even respected, she had hardly the rights of a condemned criminal. Men held her in hearty contempt: she was the least of them all, hardly worth thinking about. But her march to emancipation and a place in the sun was to start when the Eleven Men came knocking at her door, calling her out into the blazing light of that equality and freedom which the "marvelous" Roman law had for ever denied her.

Her marriage was a joke. She might be joined to her husband by a religious ceremony which meant nothing to either of them; she might become a wife by simply eating a rice-cake with a man; she might come to be considered his wife by simply living with him, after the manner of our modern "common law." One method meant no more to her than another; no matter which was used, she became the property of her mate, and sacrificed whatever rights she ever had as a maiden. She was a "thing," bought and sold and treated like any other piece of furniture in her home. Later, there was "free" marriage, which amounted to legal concubinage: the woman might live with her husband if she chose, but she kept her property separate from his, worshiped her own gods and left her husband whenever she chose.

Divorce became an open scandal. Seneca, living in the days of the Apostles, speaks of "daily divorces"; and adds that the Roman Mæcenas was "married a thousand times." Even the illustrious Cicero repudiated his wife, Terentia, in order to get out of some embarrassing debts and took Publilia to wife, only to leave her almost as unscrupulously as the other. Caius Gallus, a Roman

general, divorced his wife because he saw her walking
in the street with head uncovered. Well-born women
reckoned their years by the number of husbands they
had married and divorced: one woman had eight husbands in five years. Saint Jerome tells us of a woman
married to her twenty-third husband. Even Reno might
envy that record, and Reno is accepted only as a national
scandal where Rome was accepted as a matter of course.

The Roman mother was expected to bear children,
but to have no voice in their training, or power in controlling their behavior. They were the children and the
property of the father, not the mother. They never
dreamed of consulting her when they got ready to
marry, for they knew her as the law taught them to
know her, as a sister and not a superior, their equal and
nothing more. All her earnings and property, like those
of her children, went to her husband. He was her lord
and master, and he knew it. He did anything that came
into his mind, and he was perfectly safe in doing it.
He was the perfect example of the double standard: that
archaic doctrine that a woman can do nothing she wants,
the man everything he pleases. Greek and Latin literature is filled with the records of his shame, with traces of
unnatural vices which have utterly passed out of memory
in the Christian world. There were armies of concubines and hosts of illegitimate children. Schools of
prostitution were run under cover of the Temple of

Venus. In the theater were hordes of girls supposed to be actresses, but actually serving out lifetimes of slavery to Roman lust. Vice and immorality had reached unbelievable depths during the early reign of Constantine.

The Christian code of life set itself like a wall of flint against such standards. They opposed from the beginning the blasphemy of Roman marriage, the evils of divorce, the institutions of prostitution and concubinage and the general degraded position of women. Constantine started it in 340 when he made it illegal for married men to have concubines, and treated adultery as a capital crime. Concubinage was opposed in all its forms, and legitimacy given to all children whose parents subsequently married. Christians stayed away from the Temples of Venus, and in time those temples ceased to be; Christians stayed away from the lewd theater, set themselves against its practises, with the result that never since has the stage gone down to the depth it touched in first-century Rome.

"Nothing in human affairs is so much to be venerated as marriage," declared Constantine. That one statement might stand as his greatest monument: he made many mistakes, but he established the Christian ideal of the sanctity of the marriage bond. Not that he did it alone, he was the pioneer of a long line who gave it attention. Marriage, under the steady pressure of the new faith, ceased to be a joke. It became a bond of

equal union, the highest spiritual relationship, sealed
"in the name of the Father, and of the Son and of the
Holy Ghost." The demand for life-long faithfulness
on the part of each was an added link in the chain
which bound them. Virtue and propriety were taken
for granted when brides and grooms knelt at Christian
altars. As the church grew in power, the indissolubility
of the marriage bond was urged. A still greater spiritual
significance was attached to the sacrament when people
came to believe that the union was to continue through
endless ages of a coming life. Man and woman entered
into a sacred compact with God as their witness. This
meant not only greater dignity for the ceremony, but
also for her who had once been considered a mere object
in trade: woman, henceforth, in the eyes of the law,
stood on level ground with man.

She was protected, under Constantine, from much
of the old injustice of divorce. A law of 331 allowed
her to secure a divorce for any of three reasons: if her
husband were a "murderer, magician, or violator of
tombs." The husband might divorce his wife for
adultery or other unfaithfulness. If a woman could
prove that she had been unjustly divorced, she might
take all the property of her husband. These laws were
abolished under Justinian. In fairness we must admit
that the influence of the Christian on Roman divorce
was uncertain; the gains of one generation were lost

in the next in many matters of marriage and separation. It was not until the twelfth century that the influence gained an established foothold, when divorce was prohibited except for flagrant offenses. This change gave birth to modern legislation in favor of woman.

Woman never had a chance at these reforms under any other religion or régime. No philosophy or old faith known among the Greeks or Romans had lifted her very far from her low estate and estimate in the mind of man. Even Stoicism failed to elevate her, fine and beautiful as it was. It remained for Christianity not only to improve her legal position but to place about her that halo of respect and tenderness which is with her to this day. Jesus started it when he held out his hand to the Magdalene, making her over from a woman despised into a saint for whom we name our churches. The marching Eleven continued it when they invaded the Roman home, fought down the beastliness in man and lifted woman to a place of power and respect. Echoes of that battle were heard in the Middle Ages, in deeds of chivalry when knighthood was in flower; and in the first cry of modern shipwreck at sea: "Women and children first!"

It is often true that what was gained in one age was lost in another, and regained in the third. But the steady pressure of Christ on men and morals has never let up. It has produced a social and moral order, after

centuries of struggle, which is as much brighter than
the Roman order as day is brighter than night. Go to
India, and the Far East, and to lands where Christians
do *not* make the laws. You find there that woman is
exactly where she was in pre-Christian Rome. She has
a low, degraded position, and the men who hold her in
that place have a low, degraded, inferior civilization.
Compare the life of the Christian woman with that of
the Hindu woman, and you have the whole thing in
exact perspective. Where the Indian woman is, there
is where the other women of earth would be, had the
Eleven not marched and brought to Rome that civilization which gave birth to modern Europe and America.

If Christianity had never done anything else but this,
its presence would be justified. Lecky writes in his
History of European Morals that: ". . . Christianity . . .
has exercised so deep an influence that it may be truly
said that the simple record of three years of active life
has done more to regenerate and to soften mankind than
all the disquisitions of philosophers and all the exhorta-
tions of moralists."

But Christianity was to do more: it had only started
on its march. Rome was now tottering. The last of
the really great Emperors had passed when the body of
Marcus Aurelius was laid in his tomb; after him—the
dark. Even during his reign, the enemies of Rome were
mobilizing. Circling the seven hills, as the American

Indian later circled the white man's wagon-train, rode a motley horde of savage barbarians. They had been gathering for years, while Rome feasted and grew tired. Rome might have stopped them once, but she could not stop them now. The Dark Ages were upon her and on the world, and her doom was more clearly written in the sky than the vision of Constantine had been years before.

Little men stop trying when catastrophe looks them in the eye. Little religions give up and die when disaster comes. But Christianity did not go into a panic when the barbarians circled Rome. It went out to talk with the barbarian while Rome's soldiers stayed at home. It sent missionaries to his wild tribe, to soften him before the awful blow was struck. Meanwhile the work of mercy continued behind the walls of the doomed city, on behalf of those who were exposed to destitution. With women elevated and man's mind cleansed, the Christians turned to the foundling, to the baby thrown out into the street to die in the glare of the sun and the torrents of rain; to the prisoner in his dungeon, shut away from the light of God and the justice of man; to the soldier who wanted to drop out of the wild game of war; and to the most despised of all, the Roman slave.

Chapter V

ROME PASSES

The baby, the prisoner, the soldier and the slave! They are the hope and the poison of every people. Fine babies we must have, if we would have fine men. The prisoner we have always had, and perhaps will always have; our treatment of him tells whether we are savage or civilized. The soldier with his halo of hero-worship and the slave with his miserable chain have been the warp and woof of history. These four, backbone of the Roman Empire, were the ones to whom the coming of Christianity was as the sight of land after many weary days at sea.

When a desperate mother in New York City, in the year of our Lord 1929, left her baby on a subway bench, we who read of it could scarcely believe our eyes. That kind of behavior is front-page news, unusual in our kind of world. Something probably wrong with a mother's mind, we said, to do a thing like that. The greatest tragedy in the life of this deserting mother was that she was born a thousand years too late: had she lived in old Rome, and not in Manhattan, she would have deserted her baby with perfect ease of mind and con-

science, and still remained one of the "first ladies" of
the city. Mothers came out stealthily at night, carrying
in their arms the infants they did not want. They
were usually girls who were a nuisance in a world that
depended on the might of fighting men. They were
dropped at the foot of the Lactarian column, left without so much as a prayer or a backward glance. Out
of the shadows, as the mother turned away, swooped a
flock of human vultures toward their whimpering prey.
Witches, some of them, who wanted babies for their
weird rituals; or slave-dealers, to whom they were worth
their weight in gold; or worse still, dealers who would
train and sell them into a life of shame. Some would
be picked up by beggars, who maimed them and made
them cripples to arouse pity and collect coins on street
corners. Occasionally there joined the hideous parade
a woman of high and noble birth, seeking a baby for her
childless home, or to collect for her some belated in-
heritance. Add to these the prowling beasts and birds
of prey; supplement it with the approval of schoolmen
and governors, voiced so well by the great grammarian
Quintilian: "To kill a man is often held to be a crime,
but to kill one's own children is . . . a beautiful custom!"
In the old Roman plays, husbands ordered the slaughter
of their unborn children, and wives were rebuked for
merely exposing their babies at the column when they
should have murdered them outright. Think of this

against the background of a calloused and indifferent society, and you have in proper focus the lamentable ethic and the overwhelming odds which confronted him who said: "Suffer the little children to come unto me."

The Stoics had opposed infanticide long before Jesus had been preached in Rome; so had certain of the more humane emperors. But Stoic and emperor alike lacked power to enforce their good intentions without the influence of an aroused public mind. Morality often runs before the law; a people often prepare themselves for legislation on a reform, long before the lawyers get together. Christian influence was more than once the road-breaker for the law, and it prepared society by working quietly, unseen, within. It did exactly that with the old Roman system of child-cruelty and child-murder. When the new faith came, teaching the inestimable value of every human soul, it not only affected the thinking of the Roman mind, but it tore from the practise of infanticide the clothes of respectability and put on it the red garments of sin and shame.

The leaders of the Church, known to us as the "Church Fathers," were thundering against it almost before there was a Church. One cried out, "We have renounced your bloody spectacles (gladiatorial combats), believing that there is no difference regarding a murder and committing it . . . and we think that to expose a child is to kill him." Clement was furious over it: "Man is more cruel to his offspring than are the animals." Lactantius was ashamed for them: "They have educated their own blood for slavery or the brothel." Their rousing protests shook Rome awake, stirred in the Roman heart that latent goodness which lies deep in us all, and blazed the way for Constantine to declare in 315: "Let a law be at once promulgated in the towns of Italy, to turn parents from using a parricidal hand on their new-born children. . . . Watch and care over this, that, if a father bring his child saying that he cannot support it, one should supply him without delay with food and clothing . . . and we order that our revenue as well as our treasure aid in this expense." That wise provision should remain a monument to Constantine. He has been given little enough credit for anything he did. Lewis Browne, in his recent *Since Calvary,* dismisses Constantine and all his works with the trite remark: "It (Christianity) had climbed aboard the chariot of a tavernkeeper's grandson and had arrived. . . ." But not a word about what happened to Rome when the Cross supplanted the Roman eagle! Not even a backhand compliment to the man who, charlatan or saint, did at least this much to turn civilization and the minds of men from cruelty to love.

Constantine started what Justinian finished. He became Emperor at Constantinople in 529 and created the Code of Justinian, a system of law packed to the brim with Christian influence. This humane code was the full-blown flower grown slowly from the seed of Constantine. The abandoned infant, even if a slave, became free by the very act of abandonment. He might acquire and dispose of property, and hold the rights of a free-born Roman. Deserting parents were threatened with the direst penalties, and exposure was made to appear more brutal than ordinary murder. Justinian went further even than this. He asked the Archbishop of Thessalonica to take his church on a new crusade in behalf of the deserted infant, to throw the strength of the Church of Christ against infanticide. With such encouragement the Church threw a protecting arm around deserted childhood, and there began to spring up all over the land, those hospitals and houses-of-mercy which we of to-day take so much for granted.

Hospitals and orphanages had been built before, by Emperors worried over the declining birth-rate or the degeneracy of morals. But when Justinian looked in the direction of the Christian and said, *"You* take care of them," he started something greater than he knew. He made reverence for childhood a religious duty and not a political expedient. He started marching abreast of the Eleven Men a host of men and women in every age who have given their lives, in religious orders and charitable endeavors, to the reclamation of childhood and of youth. In France during the Middle Ages there were orphanages with a "turning-slide," or swinging door, through which were thrust the half-starved or neglected babies of desperate, poverty-stricken mothers. That swinging door evolved from a marble vessel set outside the doors of the first Christian churches in Rome, in which were placed the unwelcome strangers who otherwise would have been lost at the Lactarian column. We no longer have turning-slides nor swinging doors but nurseries, foundling homes and baby hospitals. Babies are still deserted in London, Paris and New York; but even the most desperate of mothers and the meanest of criminals abhor the practise.

Then there was the prisoner. No classic legislator ever wasted time on him. He was a criminal who had broken the law of man; or a political rebel, dissatisfied with the *status quo*; or a religious rebel, like Paul; or one who had dared to think ahead of his age. No matter what he was, he deserved to be punished. His fate was so horrible that he may well have carved over the door of his cell the legend which Dante put over the door of hell: "All hope abandon, ye who enter here." That hope was never more forlorn than in the days of pre-Christian Rome; the prisoner was never more completely forgotten than when the Roman mob was shouting at the Circus. As a candle burns brightest in the darkest room, so in the darkest hours of the prisoner's dungeon-despair there came the greatest light. He heard the creaking of a new key in his door, and the sound of a new foot-step in his prison corridor. The Eleven Men had arrived.

"Cells must have light and air," ruled Constantine. "Prisoners are not to be branded or disfigured." Men and women in later days were segregated in separate prisons, and not confined together. Criminals were no longer hustled into the amphitheater to fight the beasts; capital punishment was forbidden unless the culprit confessed, or on sworn testimony by his accusers. Judges were required, under Honorius, to visit the prisons each Sunday, to witness the infliction of the sentences they had imposed. This was a decided start toward a new day, when prisoners were to be treated as men who had made mistakes and not as animals gone mad. The fruit of that first Christian reform is modern penology: that state of mind and humanitarian science which insists that "cells must have light and air," and that "when men are treated as men they will react as men." And that may be something of an improvement over old Roman law and third-century customs!

What of the man of war, the soldier? What happened to the ambassadors of the short-sword when Peter, disarmed in Gethsemane, came to Rome? He did some disarming, but not much; he did not stop the killing, nor wipe out war. Peter's own church, in later years, was to take the sword, leave Jesus far behind, and dip her hands in the blood of men. It has been the hardest

of all fights, this fight of Christ and Mars. It was not
easy for those first disciples of the Prince of Peace to
stand against the military spirit in the very headquarters
of Roman might. But there they took their stand, often
at the cost of their own lives. The early Church was
a stubborn foe of militarism: six thousand Christian
soldiers in the Theban legion threw down their arms and
refused to fight again; six thousand heads came off, but
the arms stayed where they were. Maximilian, drafted
for a war, stood in the presence of certain death and
cried: "I am a Christian. I can not fight." Brave words
for one lone man to speak in an age of blood and iron.
Whole legions came to appreciate what Maximilian had
done, and the time came when not a solitary Christian
could be found in their ranks. One writer is so bold as
to say that for two hundred years there was not a single
Christian in the armies of Rome. Exaggerated, no
doubt, but indicative of the first real opposition to the
bloody art of war, the first signs of tarnish on the halo
of the soldier.

The opposition, however, weakened, in view of wars
and rumors of wars, and the protest was finally lost in
a fierce shout which came out of the East, from a million
Moslem throats. Mohammed, camel-driver and prophet
of Allah, was waving his bloody scimitar in the air and
screaming: "The sword is the key to heaven and to hell."
And his horde of frenzied, maddened followers echoed:

"Death to the infidels." Mohammed was building the most powerful rival that Christianity was to know, and his Moslem armies were to shake the world. In a decade Palestine, Syria, Persia and Egypt were wrested from the Christians. Within a century Asia and Africa were lost, the Islamic banner of the Crescent was raised over the birthplace of the Christ, Spain was captured, Rome was threatened and the whole Western Empire was in peril. But for the issue of a single battle, the Moslems would have conquered Europe. Charles Martel checked them at Poitiers (732) and decided thereby that Europe and the West were to be Christian and not Mohammedan. But the die was cast: the Church had taken up the sword, and could not put it down. The threat of Islam passed, but there came the reaction of resentment and revenge. For centuries Christian pulpits advocated war on the Moslem and the Turk. Its highest sanction was reached during the Crusades when, as Lecky puts it, ". . . the soldier knelt down and prayed before the Cross, (and) that cross was the handle of his sword."

The fight against war has been feeble and uninspiring. It has lagged and been retarded by economic and political influences, which have proved more potent than religious faith. But the fight has never quite died out. It blazed up again in the "Peace of God" of feudal days, in arbitration proposals and in the "outlawry of war" in our own day.

The Eleven Men did not beat into plowshares all the swords of fighting men; neither did they strike away the shackles of slaves captured by the fighters. This has been quoted as a failure of the Church, but it may be a blessing, to civilization at least, that those chains were not struck off at once. What would have happened had that multitude of slaves been granted immediate release and equality with their masters? Rome and all Europe might have been drenched in blood. The master hated and feared the slaves who served him, and whom he ruled precariously, by threat of torture and of death. The slaves longed for a chance to wrest that rod of iron from their master's hand and strike him down. They had tried it several times, and defeat only aggravated the desire for revenge.

In slave-memory lingered bloody pictures of unsuccessful rebellions and ruthless cruelties. Spartacus, the gladiator, led an uprising in 71 B.C., but he was hacked to pieces and six thousand of his rebel band were hung on crosses along the road to Rome. The rich Flaminius put a slave to death merely to amuse a guest who had never seen a man die. Cicero declared that nothing great or noble could exist in a slave. Gaius, Roman jurist under Marcus Aurelius, classified slaves as animals. Seneca the Elder said that a slave had no heart and no religion. Juvenal, greatest writer of them all, asked: "How can a slave possibly be a man?" Even the Stoics, old enemies of slavery and preachers of equality, were guilty of the most repellent tortures on their slaves.

Christianity worked no miracle on that deeply rooted thinking, nor on the institution of slavery as a whole. Some early churchmen seemed to approve of it; medieval officials held slaves to a very late date. There is nevertheless a record, nine centuries long, of legislation which granted gradual emancipation to the slave. Torture was the first to go, then slave-killing in the arena; finally the slave arrived at the place where he might hold and sell property and even hold high office. The old distinction between master and slave gradually disappeared as the Church gained control, for the contempt of one man toward another was intolerable among men who worshiped Christ.

It was something new when slaves went to church with their masters, and sat side by side through the service of prayers and hymns, and received together the sacrament of the Lord's Supper. Equality usually came only when the slave rebelled and won his freedom at the cost of blood, when he could say to his master, "I am as good as you are." Christianity reversed all this when it induced the master to hold out his hand to the slave and say, "You are as good as I am." Slaves even entered the priesthood and heard confessions from their former masters. Justinian built a beautiful church at Ravenna, and dedicated it to the memory of a martyred slave. The old contempt and the old division lines passed when slave and master alike became "one body, bond or free."

Among the other merciful influences were the emancipation of slaves on feast days of the Church, the gradual easing of their hard lot and the dignity bestowed on the humbler virtues of humility, obedience and resignation. But it all came too late. Even while these changes were taking place, there came a terrible knocking at the gates of Rome. Before the walls stood Alaric, fierce leader of the Goths, his sword thirsty for blood and his hands itching for loot. And in the army at his back were forty thousand Roman slaves, the weapons of the masters in their hands, watching— waiting——

CHAPTER VI

DARKNESS—AND A STEADY HAND

THEY had not long to wait. On the night of the fourteenth of August, 410, the last lines of defense went down, and they swarmed into the city. Those trumpets of Alaric, sounding at midnight in the streets of sleeping Rome, announced that the mighty right arm of the Empire had been broken, that this city of the seven hills was no longer impregnable nor supreme. For a week the barbarians and the ex-slaves went about their work, filling the gutters with blood and their wagon-trains with plunder. They left behind them a smoking ruin, and turned away to ravage Italy.

It was partly the fault of Constantine, dead now nearly eighty years. He had split the world and history in twain. Never popular in old Rome, he built himself a "new Rome," known to posterity as Constantinople. That new city became the seat of Emperors, saved civilization for a thousand years—and divided the forces of the Empire. But even had there been no great Constantinople in the East, Rome in the West was doomed to go down, sooner or later, before that flood of barbarian invaders from the North.

Alaric, tall and blond and a mighty chieftain, died on his return home, and was buried in the bed of a river, turned aside from its course to hide his grave. In his very shadow there came an ugly squat-faced fellow from a log hut in Hungary. He was Attila, the "Scourge of God," at the head of half a million Huns, most feared of all the scourges of that crashing world. In 450 Attila sent a terrifying note to Constantinople and to Rome: "Attila commands thee to prepare a place for his reception." Marcian, Emperor at Constantinople, sent back a daring reply: "I have gold for my friends, steel for my enemies." Rome did not answer at all, and Attila, knowing the strength of Constantinople and the weakness of Rome, turned to the West. Defeated at Chalons, he retreated across the Alps into Italy. He descended upon a Rome still staggering from the awful blow of Alaric, her armies in disorder, her people panic-stricken, her old power gone. Nothing could save Rome now.

But she *was* saved—as by a miracle. There stood at the gates of the threatened city an impressive figure resplendent in the robes of a bishop. It was Leo the Great, the first of a long line of powerful popes. The papacy was just coming into power; the Church had seized the scepter which fell from the hands of the Emperor, to hold it for centuries. No stage has ever caught or reproduced the blazing drama of Leo facing

Attila, and mediating on behalf of Rome when Rome was absolutely helpless and at the mercy of the barbarian. Awed by the majesty of the priest, smarting from his defeat at Chalons, harassed by guerrilla bands of Roman soldiers, the Hun accepted tribute instead of loot, took the trail of Alaric, burst a blood-vessel and died. It was one of the breathless moments of history: it was significant that Attila was turned back. It was still more significant that the only leadership left in Rome had been transferred from the Empire to the Ecclesia.

Leo tried to play the part of the savior a second time, and he failed. Genseric the Vandal had cut down a young forest near Mount Atlas, built a fleet of young, green-timber ships, and sailed them down to the mouth of the Tiber in 455. Leo tried to impress him as he had the Hun, but Genseric pushed him aside to strike the final crushing blow at the Eternal City. Palaces and temples, the architectural glory of the ages, were leveled with the dust. Exquisite statues and works of art, ages old and gathered from the ends of the earth, were carried out into the streets and smashed into bits. Whatever had been left standing by the gentler Alaric was destroyed by the Vandal army in fourteen days. Crowds of captives were hustled aboard the green-timber ships and sent moaning overseas to Carthage. It was the last act, the final lowering of the curtain which threw the stage of Europe into complete, impenetrable darkness.

Europe became a madhouse. Barbarian chieftains, who yesterday were nothing more than robber chiefs, supplanted the last of the weak Emperors, who went down like a reed in the wind. Puppet rulers were elevated to staggering thrones, only to be roughly pulled down again and sent off into oblivion. Back and forth in the hideous night swept the armies of the Goths, Vandals and Franks. Then came Saxons, Danes, Alemanni, Lombards and Burgundians. Some of them plundered and disappeared; others settled down amid the ruins, establishing a state of petty war and the rule of brigand and marauder. They swept into the ash-heap the last remnants of the old civilization, and but for one restraining hand they might have wiped out the last trace of all civilization. *That restraining hand, which eventually tamed the barbarian and created modern Europe, was the Christian Church. Without it, there would have been nothing but anarchy from the North Sea to the Bosphorus.*

There were two gestures to that restraining hand. One was a gesture of retreat, seen in the movements of monks and priests. They were appalled by the deepening darkness, the continuance of bloodshed, the spread of ruin. They despaired of saving the barbarian and their own people, and in that desperation they retired to the mountains and the desert that they might at least save themselves. This was the beginning of monasticism in the Church, an influence and a movement destined to be at once baneful and helpful. Out of the confusion of those days comes one great fact: the Dark Ages are remembered quite largely by the work of these men who ran away.

There was also the gesture of the helping hand. It was extended *to* the barbarian and to others in the world at large, and no one was ignored or despised. The spirit of those who practised this method is seen to best advantage in Augustine's *City of God,* where it is made plain that Christians were to save the world by building it from within.

Augustine! What a name to conjure with! He rears his leonine head like a great rock on a prairie. He is the greatest figure of all the period, the giant who laid the foundations of the Roman Catholic Church, of the philosophy of history, of more Protestant theology than Protestants sometimes care to admit. He supplied the finished apology for the papal system, fathered the doctrines of purgatory and predestination, was supreme mystic and lover of God. His *City of God* is dry reading to us, but it opened the door to those desperate churchmen of the Dark Ages who were lost and seeking a way out. They grasped at it as a drowning man grasps at a straw.

"The City of God" was the Church; it was a congregation of men who had found God, and who were to have dominion over all the earth. The monastics set themselves to achieve this ideal by methods of retreat before the foes of worldliness and social corruption. They became hermits, wanderers in desert places, practising self-inflicted punishments to keep them humble before God. Some lived in caves, or in mere holes in the ground; they dined on berries and on fruits; they never washed, nor did they change their rude clothing until it fell from their shoulders in rags. They were "ascetics," who hated even their own "wicked" bodies, and therefore would not cleanse them. In the East especially they went to absurd extremes. Saint Simon Stylites sat for thirty years on the top of a high pillar; Saint Eusebius labored about under one hundred and fifty pounds of iron chains; Saint Besarion for forty years never lay down to sleep; Saint Anthony, first and most denying of them all, was proud of the fact that "never, to extreme old age, had he been guilty of washing his feet!" A thousand forms of fanatical self-denial were followed in the frantic search for God.

Yet there was wheat in this chaff of monasticism, seen perhaps at best advantage in the career of Benedict. Here was a monk who forsook the world for the sake of saving it; he built a monastery at Monte Cassino and established in it his famous Benedictine Rule, a new broom with which he began the work of sweeping away the old fanaticisms. He halted the retreat of the would-be holy man from the world by preparing him to go back again. He discouraged laziness, and set the members of his Order to work. They made gardens, that they might feed themselves. They studied, pursued definite reading courses when the art of reading and of study had been nearly drowned out in a welter of blood. He had others write or copy manuscripts or arrange historical records. They preserved what little learning there was left, and guarded those old manuscripts and records without which we to-day would find many a missing link in the story of mankind. The first libraries of our civilization were built by them, in a day when cruder men were building camp-fires with written records. Indeed, the only teachers, artists, authors of the times were found in the shadow of the Cross. The lamp of science and literature, burning in the cell of the monastery monk, was the single dim reflection of the torch of knowledge for over five hundred years.

They were to have piety, commanded Benedict. Seven times a day they were called to prayers. They rose at midnight to sing hymns and offer up their supplications. Those midnight songs were the only sound of melody left in a world filled with discord of clashing arms. It was a faint echo of the voice of God, but it never quite died out though heard often in a minor key.

In these fortresses of God, faith smoldered, waiting to burst into flame in a more fortunate day.

Another Benedictine requirement was the practise of self-denial. They were to have nothing, want nothing, give all. In that self-denial began the transformation of what was practised by the pillar-sitters and the chain-bearers. It ceased to be selfish and became social. The monks gradually moved back into the world outside the monastery wall, to reclaim those whom they had once forsaken. In short, they began to teach: for six centuries the only schools were monastery schools.

The students, at first, were priests and monks who had found themselves in a pitiful state of ignorance. Even many of the leaders, the bishops and the abbots, did not possess the culture of a modern high-school boy. Priests could barely stammer through the words of the sacraments; any one who understood grammar was a phenomenon. They were blind, trying to lead the blind. But to their eternal glory be it said that they tried to cut the cataracts from their own eyes! They studied theology, Hebrew and Greek, in what might be regarded as the first theological seminaries. The old "dead" languages, such as Arabic and Chaldee, were taught and not forgotten. Most of the subjects studied in these early "schools of higher learning" had an ecclesiastical flavor. But the guardians of learning soon began to shed their light among the laymen.

"It hath seemed good to us that priests . . . should receive into their houses young readers to whom they give spiritual nourishment, teaching them to study. . . ." So spoke the Council of Vaison, in 529 A.D. The Synod of Orléans, in 799, said, "Let the priests in villages and towns hold schools, in order that all children entrusted to them can receive the first notion of their letters. Let them take no money for their lessons." Charlemagne decreed in 789: "Let one open schools to teach children to read; let, in every monastery, in every bishopric, some one teach psalms, writing, arithmetic, grammar, and employ correct copies of holy books."

Charlemagne! He was the grandson of that Charles Martel who stopped the Mohammedans at Tours. Like his grandfather, he was a king and a man of war; he was a better man than his grandfather in that he was a "man of letters" as well. He could actually write his own name! He sent for scholars from everywhere and gathered into his court all the learning he could find. He had scholars read theology to him as he dressed and ate breakfast in the morning; he was the greatest influence in history for lay education; he brought learning out of the monastery and scattered it across the world.

Charlemagne followed the lead of those traveling monks who were scattering the seeds of wisdom and of faith. Incredible as it may seem, some men were moving out into the burning night while their more timid brothers were seeking the shelter of the monastery. It was an age of missionary endeavor as well as of barbarian invasion. Some one had gone to Clovis, King of the Franks, and led him down into the waters of baptism. He then turned to his tribesmen and said, "You, too." It was a case of "follow-the-leader," and three thousand of them submitted to baptism, preferring to follow him rather than to die. Their action is typical of the mass conversion of other tribes, at the command of their princes. Few of them knew what it was all about. Even Clovis did not grasp it. When he heard the story of Calvary, he flew into a rage and cried: "Had I and my Franks been there, it would never have happened." In that remark is a glimpse of the heart-breaking task of the missionary who took Christ to the land of the barbarian who had been converted with a sword at his throat. He was sent out to make Christians in practise as well as in theory, in deed as well as in word. It was impossible. He did it.

The missionary was not only the herald of world-evangelism. He was the pioneer of modern education. One of the best known was Saint Patrick, who went to Ireland. Poor Patrick! We think of him as the world's premier chaser of snakes. He probably never chased one in his life. What he did do was to spend his life chasing the serpents and demons of ignorance. When he came to Ireland there was not even an alphabet. He made one and taught Ireland how to use it. He built the first schools on the Emerald Isle and became the "father of schoolhouses" in northern Europe. Between sermons he taught Irish boys and Irish *girls*. Co-education, which we consider a development of our own day, was a gift thrown into our laps by Saint Patrick and his wandering tribe of priestly schoolmasters. Women sat in his class-rooms and learned to spell and read and teach. Saint Patrick left behind him, when he died, the first of that modern host of the tender sex who are the teachers of reading, writing and arithmetic of our children.

Saint Columba baptized converts and taught them grammar in Scotland, while Saint Columban was doing the same for Gaul. Both founded all their efforts on education: they built a chain of missions, and within the missions they forged another chain—a series of in-dustrial schools. Augustine, a monk sent out by Gregory the Great, taught the common people and saved what is now England for the Christ. Boniface went to the Germans, and held up the torch that they might see. It was a race, as H. G. Wells has said of our own times, be-tween education and catastrophe. Education won in the hands of the marching missionary. Education! It is the fetish of the modern cynic, called by him the new savior of civilization come to replace religion. It was the first tool hammered out and tempered and improved in the ecclesiastical smithies of the early Church!

Charlemagne started the larger part of this movement.
He gave the peoples he conquered one choice: accept
Christianity or the sword. Those who accepted, received
missionaries to tell them what it was all about. Strange,
inconsistent procedure, that! But Charlemagne was a
strange and inconsistent man. On Christmas Day in the
year 800, he knelt at the altar of St. Peter's at Rome, a
giant figure with a giant heart and mind, the eyes of the
world upon his back. Pope Leo III came forward and
placed a crown on his massive head, to the accompaniment of shouts of "Long live Charles Augustus,
Emperor of the Romans." That was a clever move. It
was the official wedding of Church and State, delayed
since the days of Constantine. It was the creation of a
new Holy Roman Empire. It was the beginning of a
never-ending struggle for power between popes and the
kings they crowned.

The giving of crowns within the power of the Christian Church! Will it accelerate the marching of the
phantom host who follow the original Eleven Men, or
will it be an ambush full of danger and defeat? What
was to happen to Charlemagne and to those who came
after him?

CHAPTER VII

AFTER CHARLEMAGNE

THE crown sat well upon the brow of Charlemagne. The grandson of Charles Martel was to the manner born: he knew how to wear it, how to win respect for it by the sword, honor for it through the scholars at his court. As the scepter settled snugly in his grasp, and a new day settled on his world, the Middle Ages arrived. Now "Middle Ages" is a most deceptive term; roughly, they were the years from Charlemagne in 800 to Martin Luther in 1500. Called variously the Dark Ages, the Age of Chivalry, the Age of Law and the Age of Faith, it was a period of intermittent light and shadow, of shifting darkness and bewildering mist, of ugly poverty and uncounted wealth, of heroic death along the roads to Palestine and cowardly death by poison in the palaces of the Pope. The destinies of men and nations fly crazily about in the mad dice-box of fate. Europe was just coming of age, and mankind was searching eagerly for a sure footing in the drifting fog.

Out of the dim East came romantic Haroun-al-Raschid, hero of the one-thousand-and-one immortal escapades of *Arabian Nights*. In 802 he gave his friend

Charlemagne a beautiful clock, adorned with wooden
figures which moved and played musical instruments.
Haroun, like Charlemagne in the West, had built a
splendid palace at Bagdad, and filled it with poets,
scholars and scientists. The golden age of Arabian literature began with him. But that clock: it was probably
striking the fateful hours when the Saracen sons of
Haroun ravaged Asia Minor, Spain and Crete, and finally
stood at the gates of Rome in 846. It may have been
striking when the Turks marched on Constantinople.
The wooden figures had probably only ceased to march
and play when Genghis Khan, the Mongol, led his armies
deep into Russia. Those threats from the East are full of
meaning for Christian history.

Out of the sea-mists of the North came a string of
long narrow boats bearing down on the shores of the
North Sea and the Mediterranean. At the oars of those
boats sat the Viking. He was even more furious a
scourge than Attila. Blood was his passion, war his
deepest love. He and his comrade Norsemen leaped into
battle like so many unleashed tigers, certain that the
way to fame and immortality for them lay across the
heaps of their enemy dead. They asked no greater final
reward than to drink mead, in Valhalla, from the skulls
of their conquered foes. Without even a speaking
acquaintance with fear, they burned and ravaged and
plundered whatever lands their serpentine galleys could

reach. So fierce were they in reputation that people began to pray for deliverance from them: "From the fury of the Norsemen, O Lord, deliver us," is an old Gallican prayer. Only one thing they could not destroy, and that was the Christian religion which conquered them. They sailed up the Seine to Paris, across the Atlantic to find America five hundred years before Columbus paced the docks of Genoa, and they sent their wild Norse blood flowing in the veins of British sovereigns. William the Conqueror was of their strain; he called himself "Norman" instead of "Norseman," and with him England was brought into the full tide of European civilization.

Out of the dim mists of barbaric invasion and settlement, we begin to see great nations swarming, shaping up. France was being hammered out in history's forge. Some of Charlemagne's own Franks had settled in a district called Francia, near Paris, and in 987 their leader was made king of what some day was to become the kingdom of France. Spain was being reclaimed. The Christians who retreated from the Saracen and the Moor to the mountains of the North began to venture out again, to drive the infidel from their native land. Modern Germany was growing out of the "East Frankish Kingdom," and was about to be annexed to the Western Empire, named "Holy Roman Empire" by Frederick Barbarossa in the twelfth century.

But the most powerful men of the Middle Ages did not come charging out of the East nor sailing out of the North. They were neither soldiers nor princes, but priests and popes. The priests dominated the thinking and living of the medieval man, woman and child. They sat in the civil courts, taught in the classroom of the school, baptized babies into the church and the kingdom, snatched fathers and mothers out of the dread medieval hell by absolving them of their sins. They were the point of contact between the Pope, who had become God's supreme representative on earth, and the people. The Pope himself was busy at the work of controlling the temporal rulers. He placed crowns where they served his purpose of strengthening the Church, and he snatched them off when the rulers became obstreperous. Had all the later princes been Charlemagnes, there might have been no snatching of crowns. But they were of meaner, poorer stuff, and fell to quarreling over divisions of land and wealth. The popes saw in these dissensions their great opportunity to take a fresh grip on the reins of power, and the struggle was on between Ecclesia and Empire. Popes came to reign supreme, abused their power, were rebelled against and dethroned. The "Vicars of Christ" raised their own armies and went out to do battle with the secular power. There were weak popes, not fit to hold the reins: one was pulled from his throne, slapped in the face, and paraded like a clown through the streets. But strong popes also came to control affairs with energy and ability. Hildebrand forced a king to stand barefoot in the snow for three long days, begging for pardon and papal favor. Thomas à Becket was murdered in Canterbury Cathedral for opposing the King, and King John of England was forced to hand over his kingdom to the Pope. Out of that handing, incidentally, came the Magna Charta of 1215. It was in all a day of rolling bloody darkness, in which popes and kings alike forsook their Christ.

Darkness now settled down on the Church. Constantinople and Rome came to the final parting of the ways, and went their separate roads to doom. They excommunicated each other, thereby working evil only to themselves. Three popes, even four, ruled at once, and tried to kill one another. The Borgias took the Church down to the depths by way of poison and the dagger. Mere boys became bishops, and half-grown men were popes. The Inquisition arose as a tool against heresy, and became the darkest blot on the escutcheon of the Church. Orthodoxy was defended at the price of the soul. Monasteries again went down and became the hiding-places of red shame. Abbots, nuns and monks, unceasingly drunk, broke their vows of chastity and piety without the slightest blush. Masses were said to the devil; the Church struck bottom. That was the dark side, and it was very dark. We see, presently, the brighter side, in the coming of the poor little man of Assisi, who was to save religion, and in the advent of the monasteries at Cluny and Cîteaux.

Meanwhile the world outside had been splitting up. Charlemagne's great kingdom had reached its heyday, and gave way slowly to a new order known as "feudalism." The age of feudalism is that age, that interlude, between the passing of Charlemagne and the rise of the modern European nation, in which groups of petty states arose, ruled by princes under the sovereignty of kings. Dukes, counts and barons gained control of great estates of land, and worked them with bands of slaves now called "serfs." The feudal lords themselves lived in castles reared on dominating hilltops in the midst of their lands. "Feudal" is a good word, a good description of them: they fought an endless series of bloody feuds and petty wars. It was a case of prince against king, baron against baron, village against village, neighbor against neighbor.

Kings, with a war cloud looming on their horizon, would buy help and allegiance from their barons by awarding them grants of land. The barons subdivided these lands, giving them to lesser lords for help and an oath of allegiance to themselves. All the way down the line it went, until it reached the luckless fellow at the bottom. The serf was owned, body, mind and soul, by the baron under whom he served. He might stand in the field and watch the knights of his master go singing down the road to adventure and romance, but he was only a clod, the dead, thick, heavy stuff on which the whole structure of medieval society was built.

He was better off than the Roman slave, but not much. He paid oppressive and innumerable taxes; he repaired the highways and the castles of his lord; he saw his crops trampled down and ruined by the game hunts of the gentry. His food was bad, his dwelling a mere hut, his children uneducated. He hated his master and all other masters. It was an intolerable situation, which could never continue.

Among the great contributing causes which helped to free the feudal serf were gunpowder, the printing press and the Eleven Men. Gunpowder blew the medieval world wide open, and put into the hands of the serf a more powerful weapon than the sword and spear of the knight. Heavy costly armor, so difficult to procure, meant nothing when an enemy could shoot through it at five hundred yards. But gunpowder did not do it all, for it cost money and could be had only by the man with a fat purse. The printing press gave the serf the benefits of new learning and offered an opportunity for propaganda among his fellow serfs. But even printing presses were often searched out and smashed. They were, moreover, useless unless intelligent men could be found to work them, and intelligence was not a serf commodity. Still the leaven in the lump of society was the growing power of the Christian ideal of equality and freedom, the persistent feeling, backed by the printing press, that all men are entitled to an equal chance in life. The Christian emphasis on brotherhood came to the despairing masses like a message from on high, and they began their march, tortuously slow at first, out of the mists toward freedom. It was a progress by evolution and revolt, both of which were quickened by the growing belief that serfdom could not be reconciled with the teachings of Christ.

This achievement of freedom was strenuously opposed. The Church, for instance, following the economic trend of the times, had become a powerful owner of land and serfs. And yet the work of emancipation and elevation began as soon as Christianity gained power and control. Pope Gregory the Great, before Charlemagne, proclaimed that "Insomuch as the Redeemer of men had taken upon Himself humanity, to restore us to liberty, so it becomes us to restore those men whom nature had made free . . . to their natural condition, namely, liberty." Muratori, one of the outstanding historians of the period, flatly declared: "The great moving force in bestowing freedom upon the serf is the love implanted by the Christian religion." Masters took a torch in one hand and a servant by the other and marched around the altar of a church, thereby setting the servant free. A countess granted freedom to a female attendant, exclaiming: "Thus, we who are formed of the earth, in like manner ought to pity our fellow creatures, . . . and whatever hath been bequeathed to us, we ought to make free." Wills of dying men granted freedom to thousands, and are filled with such phrases as: ". . . for the lessening of my sins, I free thee:" "bond and free are one in Christ;" "forgive, and it shall be forgiven." The Emperor Sigismund wrote: "It is an unheard of thing that in the holy Christianity one should be so proud as to say to a man, 'Thou art mine.'" Saint Louis of France was famous for his efforts to abolish mortmain. Christian II of Denmark became known as "the friend of the serf," and forbade "the wicked and unchristian selling and giving away of free peasants." Sir Thomas Smith, writing in England, as late as the reign of Queen Elizabeth, shows the gradual effect of the pressure of Christianity: "The change of religion to the more gentle and more equal sort . . . caused this whole kind of servile servitude and slavery to be brought into that moderation so that they almost extinguished the whole. This persuasion hath engendered through the Realms a doubt; a conscience and a scruple, yet necessitie hath kept a figure or fashion thereof." Christianity did not wipe out serfdom in a day, but undermined it by creating a condition of thinking in which it could not thrive.

The effort to raise the standard of living for the lower

classes was also to be seen in the Church approval and support of the guild movement. There were guilds of silversmiths, cloth-makers and weavers, carpenters and merchants and masons, and Muratori traces their origin directly back to the Christian missionary who was the peace-maker in medieval trade disputes. When the builders and craftsmen gathered to start work on the famous Chartres Cathedral in France, one of the requirements for membership in their guilds was that the candidate must confess and be reconciled to his enemies! Such a clause might be hard to find in the agreements of modern trade unions or in the apprentice papers of young men about to become carpenters, electricians and ironworkers. Yet we may draw a straight line back from them to the guild worker of the Middle Ages, and on back to one who dignified and ennobled labor in a carpenter shop in Nazareth, and whose word that "The laborer is worthy of his hire," has steadily lifted this man from contempt to honor in the eyes of his fellows.

In those rough days, on rare occasions, serfs and lords went traveling, and in doing so they took their lives in their hands. They were in just about the position of a white explorer in the African jungle: objects of suspicion, the lawful prey of the first savage tribe to seize them. "A man is a wolf to the man he does not know," said Plautus the Roman, and his words were almost law in the Middle Ages. With the roads filled with robber bands, with barons plundering and stealing lands and wealth from one another, no strange face was to be trusted. The stranger might be a spy, a runaway, a thief, a vagrant, or a plain disturber of the peace. Even under Charlemagne, he might be seized and tortured on the bare suspicion of a crime. He could not settle among the Salian Franks if even a single Frank raised objection. In England, a stranger accused of crime must at once be confined in jail; if he were found "off from the four main roads and making no noise of bell, he could be killed as a thief." He was taxed, blackballed when he tried to establish a business, sold into virtual slavery when he could find no patron or defender. In Germany he might reside two nights as a guest, and on the third night his host assumed all responsibility for him. "Two nights a guest, the third night a servant," was the common phrase. In France the stranger living a year and a day on French soil and not professing citizenship, was made a serf to the seigneur on whose lands he resided.

The lot of these strangers was easy compared with the lot of those who followed the sea and became the victims of shipwreck. In all ages before Christianity, shipwrecked sailors or passengers were held to be the slaves of those who rescued them, and their property was confiscated. It got to be a profitable business. Ships were deliberately steered off their courses toward the rocks by false signal lights at night!

Our Eleven Men tore those rules and customs into bits and introduced practises which increased safety in travel and security of person.   Charlemagne, in 803, issued a law that strangers within his realm "should not be refused hospitality."   Alfred the Great of England, known to fame because as a youth he allowed a house-wife's cakes to burn and got his ears boxed for his care-lessness, ordered that strangers and travelers be let alone, "in memory of the Lord's people being strangers in the land of Egypt."   Each of Alfred's successors repeated this injunction on religious grounds.   The Bavarians of the twelfth century quoted the Bible against vexing the stranger, and laid a heavy fine on those who plundered or wounded the foreigner.   Old Hungarian laws called forth humane treatment for the stranger, repeating the words: "I will have mercy and not sacrifice."

The shipwrecked likewise obtained relief.   The Visi-goths, early influenced by Christianity, were among the first to introduce laws which did away with the old practise of enslaving sailors.   An Anglo-Saxon law of 978 proclaimed: "Let every merchant-ship have frith (peace) . . . let these men and what they bring with them have peace."   Henry I allowed any who escaped shipwreck to keep his goods.   Richard II declared that he did "for the love of God and the salvation of his soul demand safety and protection for all shipwrecked per-sons and their goods in whatever land or sea."   The Code

D'Oleron, just before the fourteenth century, suggested one form of punishment that is worth our notice: "Any one putting up false lights ought to be bound in the midst of his house and fire to be set to its four corners and be burned with it, and the whole place turned into a hog-yard." And even though the punishment was not more hideous than the crime, this legislation indicates the influences of the principle of Christian hospitality in an age of brute force. Some may doubt the miracle of Jesus stilling the tempest on Lake Galilee, but here is evidence enough for any doubter that Christ has worked the greater miracle of stilling the tempests of hatred, lust and cruelty in the breasts of men.

On a bitter January afternoon in 1926, a life-boat dropped over the side of the steamer *Roosevelt*, and started through mountainous seas to the sinking *Antinoe*. In that boat were a dozen men of a dozen different races, going to rescue they knew not whom. Here is dramatic contrast: think on the one hand of strangers in peril of their lives simply because they were strangers, or foreigners exposed to suspicion and slavery, or ships lured on the rocks in the Middle Ages, and on the other hand of those twelve volunteers in the tossing life-boat from the *Roosevelt*, products of a civilization which has been teaching since Calvary that "greater love hath no man than this, that he lay down his life for his friend," offering to lay down their lives for a handful of strangers.

CHAPTER VIII

PEACE AND JUSTICE

SUPPOSE we sit for a moment in the window of some medieval castle and look down upon the procession of men traveling the road past our door. Trudging along in his ragged jerkin is a stolid serf, mumbling certain incoherent words to the sickly lad at his heels. In the distance comes the caravan of a merchant from Paris or Rouen, with a battalion of guards to protect him from highwaymen. A traveling juggler is performing in the courtyard while children and white-faced women look on and laugh. And everywhere is heard the clank of armor. Knights with their ponderous swords and yeomen with their bows swarm past each other on the road, or lie at ease before the drawbridge at every castle. No matter whom else we meet, we are sure to meet the man of war. It was his armed arrogance which the followers of Christ had to face and win over in that medieval world. It followed as the night the day that Christ and Mars must meet and fight, with the souls of men as their prize.

The mailed fist was everywhere, ready to strike at the slightest provocation. Any one who thought himself

wronged had the right to send a formal challenge of war
to his enemy. Did a baron resent the behavior of a
knight serving a neighbor baron? Then to war, and
settle it with the sword. Did one family dislike the re-
marks of another? Then to battle, and wipe out the
insult with blood. Whole towns and cities followed this
method, for their charters granted them the privilege.
The Count von Solms killed the sheep of a cook of Epp-
stein, and the cook declared war. A nobleman declared
war against the city of Frankfort because a lady residing
there had promised a dance with his cousin, and had dared
to leave him and dance with another! A baker of the
Count Palatine defied three cities; the shoeblacks of
Leipzig University formally challenged the Provost of
the City. The Margrave of Brandenburg had a method
all his own, and boasted loud and long that he had
burned one hundred and seventy villages. That was the
world out there beyond your castle window: a world
torn by petty wars, in which serf and vassal suffered
most, and it seemed impossible that any form of law and
order could survive.

But look! another traveler is coming down the road.
He may be a monk, or village priest, or even a majestic
figure in the robes and miter of a bishop. The juggler
stops his nonsense, the serf halts in his tracks, the knights
look on half-curious and half-angry as the wandering
preacher gathers his motley flock about him and starts

to preach. His subject is peace, the "Peace of God," and he has preached it from town to town, nation to nation, across the length and breadth of Europe. It is a voice crying in the wilderness, or in what might have been wilderness again had the warring barons been allowed to destroy one another. This is the most superstitious age of history, and holy relics are carried about from one market-place to another, and on them wild nobles swear their vows of (temporary) peace. Bishops hold great mass meetings, lift their crosses toward the sky in eloquent appeal, and lead the people in crying, "Peace, peace." Companies of pilgrims, with white bands around their necks, travel through fourteenth-century France, praying that wars might cease. Fanatical strangers appear in the streets at dead of night, shrieking for the Prince of Peace while the horizon is red with burning towns. Pope, Church Council and local church take up the cry, and with the help of harassed merchants and worried kings, make the only attempt of these centuries to bring order out of chaos. The attempt at once succeeded and failed.

The Peace of God was intended, at first, only to protect the non-combatants and the weak. Churches, monasteries, pilgrims and the clergy were to be unmolested; so were strangers, women, children and the poor. The ox-cart, the cattle and the grain of the serf were made as sacredly inviolable as the altar of the church. But soon fighting itself came under the ban. Whole companies of barons came together and signed the articles of peace put before them by the bishop, declaring that they would not engage in fighting on the Feast Days of the Church, during Lent and Advent, and in many cases for several days of the week. A typical agreement, drawn up and signed by a roisterous, cursing company of these bearded robber-chiefs, might read: "From Thursday evening, among all Christians, friends or enemies, neighbors or distant, peace must reign till Monday at sunrise. During these four days and nights there must exist complete security, and every one can go about his own affairs in safety from all fear of enemies, under protection of this truce and peace. Let those who observe this be absolved by the Father All-powerful, by Jesus Christ His Son and by the Holy Ghost. Let those who have promised truce and who have voluntarily broken it, be excommunicated by God. Let these be accursed for ever, damned as Dathan and Abiram. Let him be banished, let him depart from Jesus. . . ."

Such agreements were voluntary; there was no compulsion, and every one signed in full knowledge of what he was doing. But heaven help him, after he had signed, if he did not keep his word. All the thunders and wrath of law and religion came down on his unworthy head. The Church made him an outcast, anathematized and excommunicated him, and after death refused him Christian burial. This may mean little to us, but it was the difference between life and death, despair and hope, for the man of the Middle Ages. To be excommunicated was the most terrible of all punishments. It meant not only the loss of the help and comfort of the Church in this life, and of the means of livelihood, but also being condemned to the everlasting flames of hell in the next. Clergy and laity turned against the violator of the Peace and he stood in immediate danger of losing his property, or his right hand, and above all the respect of his fellows.

The Peace of God, we say, both succeeded and failed. Inasmuch as fighting was the sport and business of the Middle Ages, and the Church herself quite frequently took hold of the sword, it can not be said that there was complete success in driving Mars from the earth. On the other hand, the Peace of God as promulgated by the Church did, repeatedly, stop many petty wars and fightings. Indeed, they were the only attempt at peace during those seven hundred years. The amazing thing is not that it failed to conquer war entirely, but that it succeeded at all, or that it was even tried in such an age.

It is often said, glibly and ignorantly, that the Church has always been over-cautious in introducing reform, that she has proved more adept at following than at leading in the great forward movements of history. Here at least this is not true: the great "crime" of the Church is not that she allowed wars to keep on after the Peace of God was forgotten, but that the Church was thinking too far ahead of her age. Civilization was not ready for peace. Men wanted loot, not justice. They got it. And in the midst of the furious scramble for it, the only asylum to those threatened by the seekers of loot was that offered by the Church of Christ; the only sanctuary left was the hilltop monastery. There they found no distinction between high-born and low-born, rich and poor. There they found not chaos but sound law and just government; there they met teachers who taught that they had a common Father in heaven and a common humanity on earth, instructors in the principles and technique of a new knowledge, and early scientists groping for the scientific truths which have since become the basis of our modern inventions. Such monasteries, such a Church, were the great witnesses against feudalism and the feudal caste, keeping alive, as Kingsley has it, "the sacred fire of modern liberty . . . when all the world was doing its best to trample it out." Nor were they merely the jealous guardians of liberty, learning and invention behind their monastery walls: they drained miles of swamps and acres of forests, producing tillable and fertile soil for future generations, upon which were built towns with corporate rights, middle and artizan classes, and with governments based upon monastery ideas. Representative government was taught and practised in the monasteries long before it was in the State. The Church, truly, was ahead of her age.

Other benefits of which we are the heirs may be traced back to these medieval efforts against war. The protection of the non-combatant has its modern counterpart in international law. Our humane treatment of the prisoner of war and the wounded may have been born in the days when knights were bold and chivalry was rife. Modern preachers of the Peace of God may be seen in Florence Nightingale and the Red Cross nurse. Out of it, also, came arbitration.

Late in the Middle Ages, in 1093, a group of German nobles gave the Peace a new form. They met to settle their disputes on paper, to arbitrate rather than to fight, and they made a peace that lasted for two years. In 1103, a group of bishops and nobles and the Emperor arbitrated a peace of four years' duration. In other words, the Germans did first what other nations did later: where the Peace of God failed, they established courts of arbitration, known as *Austrage*. The feuds of barons, the quarrels of peasants, and even the contests of cities were submitted to these courts, which were manned by the clergy and often presided over by the bishops. *Austrage* nearly wiped out private war in Germany, and it combined with self-interest and mercantile society to do the same in Italy and Spain. The Austragal Court of the later German Confederation is the child of these first bishops' courts. We in the twentieth century saw some of the fruits of their work but a short time ago, when the statesmen of fifteen great world powers met and solemnly declared that they would never again settle their disputes *except by pacific means.* The Kellogg-Briand Treaty, the World Court, Geneva and the League of Nations—from whence came they all? From schoolmasters, philosophers, scientists, or—priests?

Suppose now we have left our casement-window, and find ourselves in a court of law. Suppose we find there a man accused of stealing, or of failure to pay a debt, or of murder. This man and his accuser could choose between two methods of trial. They might accept the verdict of the court in a regular judicial procedure, or they might choose "wager of battle." If either had any confidence whatever in his strong right arm, he was likely to choose the latter, and challenge his opponent to fight it out on the "field of honor." This, the people in the courtroom would tell you, was perfectly just. Is not God always on the side of the innocent? Will He not cause the guilty to fall, and protect the unjustly accused? And so they go off to fight. If the accused went down, he was guilty beyond appeal. But if his *accuser* was beaten, he might be deprived of his lands, or be thrown into jail, have his right hand or his head cut off. A simple and a quick method, and it persisted for a long

time in the law-codes of Europe; there are even survivals
of it in some codes of the United States.   It may sound
ridiculous and barbaric to us, but the method was allowed
in England so late as 1818, according to the statute books.
A man acquitted of murder was challenged by the fiery
brother of the victim, because the accused had pleaded:
"Not guilty, and I am ready to defend the same with my
body."   The judge admitted the legal right of the challenge, and but for the withdrawal of the challenger, the
world would have seen a wager of battle in the nineteenth century, before the Lord Chief Justice of England.

Christianity opposed it from the start.   Saint Agobard
of Lyons, as early as 826, claimed that "It is a foolish and
proud presumption to suppose that the Divine Judg-
ments can be manifested by battle. . . ." Christian
kings and nobles ruled against it in the spirit of Alphonso
the Wise of Castile, who called it "an effort to tempt the
Lord our God."   The use of "champions" or hired
fighters in these duels early earned the scorn and contempt of the Christian.   The same determined opposition arose against them and their trade as was shown
against the gladiatorial combats, years before, in Rome.
Wager of battle was slow in dying, but it finally ceased,
not so much through process of law as by the turning
against it of the Christian mind.

Such was the influence of Christ on the wars, quarrels

and petty disputes of medieval man. The self-destructive centrifugal forces of feudalism were doubtless stayed little enough. Yet the only restraint laid upon those tyrannical tendencies came out of the strong centralized power of the Church. Christianity deliberately fought to rid the world of the blood feud, wager of battle and blood revenge. Incidentally she gave impetus and strength to a new campaign of romance known as chivalry.

CHAPTER IX

CHIVALRY

CHIVALRY! It is a glorious word from an inglorious root. It is derived from the French *cheval*, meaning "a horse." That may not be so inglorious, after all, for the word and the institution reach back to (and mayhap beyond) the rampant, dangerous days of tilts and tournaments and Round Tables, when knights rode abroad on their chargers sheathed in heavy armor, with the feather or the kerchief of some fair lady fluttering from lance or helmet. That adventurous knight of the old days has been lost all too long in the labyrinth of historical fact and fancy. He has been overshadowed, outnumbered by the ruffians and criminals of the Crusades. Minstrelsy and poetry have clothed him heavily in incredible legend; but behind that tapestry of folk-song and ballad stands the knight of chivalry, a veritable marvel of Middle Ages history. He was a new kind of warrior, turned from booty raids to unselfish quests. He was the old killer made over, spiritualized by the Christian ideal, and dedicated to mercy, courtesy, honor. Sprung from the same breed and "dragon's tooth" as his ancestor, the Roman legionnaire, there is between the two a vast difference; even like that between Mozart at the piano and the slinking hyena in the jungle. Something happened to the medieval soldier when he felt upon his shoulder the touch of the eleven marchers out of Galilee.

The man dedicated to knighthood walked in a soft glow of beauty, romance and unselfishness from the day he began his knight-apprenticeship until the day he died. At seven or eight he became a page, and as such the servant of the lady of some great mansion or estate. He ran errands for her, followed her in her walks, attended her whenever she journeyed away from home, learned from her the first rules of courtesy and the first doctrines of religious faith. At fourteen he became a squire, and carried the weapons or cared for the horses and the armor of his master. As squire he was allowed to wear a belt and sword, which came to him from the hands of a Christian priest. That entrance of the priest into the picture of chivalry was significant: The introduction of religion into the ceremonies of chivalry gave the system its greatest strength. The touch of the priest on the steel blade of the knight robbed medieval warfare of half its horror, and put courtesy and honor in the place of brutality and vice.

At Christmas, Whitsuntide or Easter the squire might become a knight after a long and brilliant religious ceremony. He fasted, confessed all his sins and passed a night of lonely vigil upon his knees before the candles of some cathedral altar. He then bathed, put on a white robe and a red, symbols of purity and the blood he was to shed for Him who died upon the Cross, and finally a flowing robe of black, to remind him of the death for ever stalking at his side. Next morning he went to mass, where he listened to a solemn discourse on the duties of knighthood, and receiving his sword or lance, took his final vows.

Those vows were different. The candidate promised "never to fight with more than one against one," nor in an unjust cause, nor to fight a man more poorly armed than himself. He was to avoid all appearance of fraud and deceit, and promised always to "conduct a lady or a maiden whom he might meet in danger to a safe retreat, serve her, protect her, and save her from all danger and all insult, or die in the attempt. . . ." "I made them," says the good King Arthur, in the *Guinevere* of Tennyson:

"I made them lay their hands in mine and swear
To reverence the King, as if he were
Their conscience, and their conscience as their King,
To break the heathen and uphold the Christ,
To ride abroad redressing human wrongs,
To speak no slander, no, nor listen to it,
To honor his own word as if his God's,
To lead sweet lives in purest chastity, . . ."

Arthur and his Round Table may be a cross-section of

that mythical and mystical tapestry of legend, but those
Arthurian vows, or similar ones, were taken by multitudes of men, only a few of whom are known by name.
Greatest of all chivalrous hearts was the Chevalier
Bayard, who took the sword from the hands of his own
mother and listened as she charged him: "Serve God
and He will aid thee. Be loyal in word and deed. Keep
thy word, be helpful to the poor and the orphan. . . ."
So thoroughly did Bayard keep his vows that he refused
to forage in an enemy's country even though the rules
of war allowed it. So completely chivalrous was King
Edward of England after the battle of Calais that he
insisted upon sitting down to supper with the captured
French knights, and in honoring above all others the
one who had nearly killed him in the fight. And Godfrey of Bouillon showed his chivalry toward Christ when
he refused to wear a crown in Jerusalem. The gentle
Saint Louis, hero of another Crusade, would "do no con-
scious injury to any man." He has been called "by the
highest standards, a Christian gentleman." "Christian"
and "gentleman" seem to go well together.

War was thus humanized by the touch of Christ, and
the hapless victims, the prisoners and the wounded,
escaped many of the savage cruelties of a former day. It
is outside the realm of sword and lance, however, that we
must look for the genuine benefits of Christian chivalry.
Not only were prisoners of war ransomed instead of

slaughtered or enslaved, but peaceful men and women were freed from oppressive tradition and the degrading rules of custom.   Over the castles of noble knights and dames were placed great ornamental helmets, inviting any traveling knight or lady to enter there and accept the comfort of food and fireside.   Hospitality became a new unwritten law, and every castle became what once only the Church or monastery had been: a refuge and a sanctuary from the harsh world beyond its doors.   We no longer place a helmet on the chimney-top, but we do write "Welcome" on our door-mats, and hold as low and mean the man who refuses aid or comfort to the stranger.

Friendship was raised to the status of a virtue, and the emphasis on loyalty and honorable conduct between men reached greater heights in those dark days than ever before.   King Arthur of the Round Table was troubled more by the treachery of Sir Lancelot than by the faithlessness of his queen.   That was because Lancelot and Arthur lived under a system in which a man's word was his bond, inviolable and worth more than its weight in gold.   The vow of friendship was a sacred thing under chivalry, as expressed in the phrase *noblesse oblige*.   No man was considered noble who could not sacrifice in order to oblige, or to whom gratitude and sincerity were not the highest laws.

Much as chivalry did for men, it did still more for women.   Beginning where Christianized Roman law left off, and aided by the high conceptions of German thought which invaded Europe with the Teutons, it placed woman on the highest pedestal she had ever occupied. That was the age when the adoration of the Virgin Mary was at the core of worship. Faith in the Middle Ages can scarcely be explained without the presence of the mother of Christ, who was exalted as "Queen of heaven and Empress of hell." Saint Monica, the mother of Augustine, was venerated in some quarters almost as much as her famous son. The mothers of Bernard, Anselm and Abelard were devoted women, in whose eyes their famous offspring first saw the gleam of God, and who put themselves for ever in civilization's debt by placing the hands of their brilliant sons in the very hand of God. Most colorful of them all was the farm girl of Domremy, who had her visions and heard the voices of her saints in her farm-garden and who at seventeen years of age went out to lead the united armies of her native France. The modern psychologist may see in Joan of Arc only a good "case" for psychoanalysis, and he may reduce her motives and her actions to mere "hallucinations, inhibitions and repressions," but those who followed her in the perilous days of chivalry saw more in her than that. She was equally impressive when clad in mail at the siege of Orléans, or when reaching for the Cross as the flames roared about her at the stake in the market-place of Rouen. Joan was the symbol, the goal of the spiritual quest of Medieval France. "In her," says Professor Nagler, "was unveiled a nobility, a public usefulness, self-sacrifice and loving service such as any age might covet." The Church has now canonized her as "Saint Joan." But the Church was tardy. The Maid had already been canonized in the rough hearts of the veterans who fought her wars, and who were so amazingly ready to trust their lives and the destiny of their France to this peasant girl. In a previous age she would have been the prey and sport of any riotous French soldier who happened to come her way. Joan is a victory for chivalry.

The Maid, Saint Monica and the Virgin are, *par excellence,* illustrations of the most prominent triumph of Jesus in the Middle Ages, and of the most far-reaching reform ever accomplished by those who followed Him; namely, the new regard for woman and the ennobling of the marriage vow. The wedding ceremony became a full-fledged sacrament, and the married woman was consecrated to sacred duties as wife and mother. The morals of womankind, single and married, were purified. Generally, the tender sex was made more worthy of the glorification they had begun to inspire. Christianity linked with chivalry went deep in protecting woman by sacrament and law from masculine caprice, and in sowing in the hearts of man and woman the seeds of comradeship. Christian chivalry made of woman the personification of beauteous virtue and the goal of romantic love, and it dignified man as the seeker after that love and the protector of that virtue.

Chivalry died as an institution with the coming of a new warfare, when the heavy suit of armor became as useless as the bow and arrow. Fair ladies throwing roses to the strong knight of the tournament might be romantic enough, but if anything in the world were unromantic and ridiculous, it was the sight of that strong knight, unhorsed, lying helpless on the ground, held motionless by his heavy suit of iron clothes. The comedy was completed by gunpowder and the cannon-ball, which unseated any number of "iron men" at one shot, and at a safe distance.

Gunpowder was democratic. Chivalry had been feudal. That is, chivalry was a class movement, the product and method of the noble, powerful and rich. Poor men and often, alas, poor ladies, suffered sometimes where those of the upper classes were protected and revered. Gunpowder was a leveler, making the chivalric code the equipment of all classes, bringing chivalry down into the common heritage of gentlemen. Armor rusts in our museums, and we stare at it and smile. But chivalry is a memory which stirs the heart like a trumpet, an envied accomplishment of the real gentleman of modern times, be he pauper or prince. The most common gesture of our civilization is that of man tipping his hat to woman.   He does that on the assumption that every woman is a lady, entitled to his respect.   And his gesture is but a different form of the practise of the "gentle perfect knight" who lifted the visor of his helmet to talk with *his* lady.   Both are products of chivalry, though one wears clothes of wool and the other clothes of steel.

Sir Philip Sidney, living and fighting in medieval days, took a cup of water from his own bleeding lips and held it to the lips of a wounded private soldier, wounded worse than he.   Ulysses S. Grant, three hundred years later, refused to take as lawful plunder the horses of the surrendered Confederates, saying that "they would need them for the spring plowing."   Marshal Foch, in the Armistice of 1918, refused to prolong the war another day, while half the world urged him to "go on and get even with the Germans."   Foch, Grant, Sir Philip, Bayard, Godfrey of Bouillon—can you follow the line back to Calvary and the Man who prayed for His enemies?   There may be some doubt in this world as to why we behave like human beings, but there should be little doubt that most men act like gentlemen because Christ and Christian chivalry have played so great a part in the molding of their character.

At the height of chivalry, a ridiculous figure rides into the scene.   Alone, on a sparebones mule, rides Peter the Hermit, preaching the First Crusade.

Chapter X

THE ROAD TO PALESTINE

PETER was even more of a sparebones than his mule. Emaciated and haggard from his weary journeys and long fasts in his hermit-cell, he traveled barefoot and bareheaded, staggering under the weight of an enormous crucifix. His eyes were smoldering coals, set in dark pits in his scraggly head. People ran after him as they run to a fire. His wild preaching drew those who had not seen his eyes, and his message threw them all into a frenzy.

He had just returned from Palestine, the Hermit said. He had been spat upon by the infidel Turk, whose flag was waving over the homeland of the Lord. He was taxed by them as he entered Jerusalem, robbed by them as he walked the streets, visiting as a pilgrim the places made sacred by the labors of Jesus. The Holy Sepulcher was in ruins, completely destroyed; it would not be long, he said, before the last holy shrine would be wiped out. Peter screamed for the vengeance of God and the sword of the Christian to drive out the Moslem and rescue the Holy Land. Europe listened, and mutterings began to be heard in every hut and palace.

Urban II, Pope at Rome, heard of the strange preacher, and his heart skipped a beat. Just what he had been waiting for! Urban was having a hard time, clinging furtively to a dancing throne which never had been wholly his. The warring of the feudal barons had challenged his authority and disrupted his fine schemes; he had fought a desperate battle to hold his waning power. The Peace of God had not brought genuine peace, and the "Truce of God," tried later, was likewise failing. Crafty, shrewd and anxious, Urban saw in the smoldering fires started by the Hermit a rare opportunity to put all the fighting men of Europe under the papal banner.

Then, too, Alexis, Emperor at Constantinople, was so hard pressed by the Turk that he was appealing to Rome for help. Urban would like to help Alexis—and thereby bring the East as well as the West beneath the dominion of Rome. Here was one chance in a million to reunite the Church. Urban hurried over across the Alps, planning secretly to meet his leading prelates and lay lords at a council in Clermont, France. They were there when he arrived: bishops, archbishops and priests without number. There were as well poor old men and rich young rulers, knights and cowards and pilgrims from Normandy who had fallen before the fire of the Hermit. Urban got them all together at one great mass meeting, had Peter preach to them, and when the fires of hatred began to glow, stepped forward himself to push Europe into the bonfire of a holy war.

"Ye men of the Franks!   [How much that sounds like Paul on Mars Hill: "Ye men of Athens!"]   An accursed race, estranged from God, has invaded the lands of the Christians in the East and has depopulated them by fire and steel and ravage. . . . These Turks have led away many Christians, captives, to their own country, they have torn down the churches of God everywhere, or used them for their own rites.   The invaders befoul the altars.   They stable their horses in these churches. Even now the Turks are torturing Christians, binding them and filling them with arrows, or making them kneel, bending their heads to try if their swordsmen can cut through their necks at a single blow. . . ." Then he got in his master stroke, bringing the threat of the Turk to their very doors: "The time may come when you will see your wives violated and your children driven off before you as slaves out of the land."   Angry shouts came up to him, but he drove on: "Come forward to the defense of Christ.   O ye who have carried on feuds, come to the war against the infidels!   O ye who have been thieves, become soldiers!   Fight a just war. . . ."   He offered protection for their property while they were away, free penance for their sins, sure salvation to every man who fell on the field of glory. "Take up your arms, valiant sons, and go.   Go with

One who lacks not the power greater than wealth to aid you. God guiding you. . . ."

He got no further. The first shouts of rage and indignation swelled up in a great wave. "God wills it!" thundered the crowd. Knights of fame pushed through to Urban and threw their swords at his feet. Paupers out of the gutters and spendthrift sons of the wealthy moved through the crowd, sobbing "God wills it." Women wept and shoved forward their sons toward the masterly Pope. Cardinals, bishops and priests worked furiously pinning on the shoulders of the volunteers little crosses of red cloth.

Barons gave their lands to the Church, freedom to their serfs, and hurried to enlist. Raymond of Toulouse, blue-blooded, scarred veteran of the Moslem wars in Spain, was among the first. Before him came Godfrey of Bouillon, with the blood of Charlemagne in his veins, to take the Cross. With them came a multitude of unknown and lesser men. Among them were criminals, adventurers, ruffians, the rabble and the shame of the Crusades, anxious for absolution and a new chance at Heaven—and the rich plunder of the East.

With the first melting of the snows in the spring of 1096, the first mad and aimless rush was on. A rabble army of three hundred thousand men, women and children, with their furniture piled high on creaking wagons, started for "Palestine," singing as they bumped

along: "God wills it!" Wives and courtezans rode the
wagons; dirty faced youngsters drove the cattle and
the sheep. They had not the least idea where Palestine
was: ten miles from home they began inquiring in every
town: "Isn't this Jerusalem?" Out in front stalked the
two Pied Pipers of a mistaken Crusade: Peter the Hermit
and an unknown soldier called Walter the Penniless,
leading the rabble straight to—death.

It was pitiful, that first advance. Disease and exposure tore at their ranks, and killed them off by the
thousand. Their only real "battle" turned out to be
a massacre of the Jews in Germany. Retaliation fell
upon them in Bulgaria and Hungary, where more
thousands died. A mere handful reached Constantinople, where they ventured too far away from the
kindly walls and were cut to pieces by the Turks.

Scarcely were the last of them dead when there came
the real soldiers of the First Crusade. Godfrey and
Raymond, old soldiers who might have saved them;
Hugh of France and Robert of Normandy; haughty,
impetuous and chivalrous Tancred, and mighty Bohe-
mund of Tarentum. These were more fortunate or
more strategic. With them was a real army of half a
million, which however dwindled away in death as snow
dies in the hot sun. Behind them, as they marched, the
road was white with their fallen dead. Yet they stormed
Nicæa and Antioch, and stood on Christmas Eve, 1099,

watching the swarming Moslems on the battle-towers
of the walls of Jerusalem.   For five terrible weeks they
drove their battering-rams at the stubborn walls, and
finally broke through to massacre seventy thousand
Moslems.   The horses of the Crusaders were up to their
fetlocks in blood.   Gentle Godfrey and magnanimous
Tancred tried to stop the butchery, but only the setting
sun saw the sheathing of the sword.   It was a human
slaughter-house, in which was vented the rage and disappointment of the terrible three-year trek across the
desert.   It was revenge for the whitening bones they
had left behind them on the march.

Godfrey ruled at first as Protector of the Holy
Sepulcher, for a single year before he died, refusing
though he ruled to wear a crown in the city where "his
Lord had worn the thorns."   This Kingdom of Jerusalem was supported by two great military orders, the
Hospitallers of Saint John and the Knights Templar.
Strange it is that the Hospitallers should be so named in
such a day, and stranger still that they should be con-
nected with a "hospital" in a day when massacre was
law.   The Red Cross nurse of our last war carried on
her breast the crimson cross handed on to her by these
first Hospitallers.   The Knights Templar of modern
times, who stage their parades in our city streets, carry
no swords of offense and revenge.   Theirs is a crusade
more genial and their methods make for tolerance and

understanding, rather than for bitterness and enmity. They are one department of the march of Christian civilization.

The Kingdom of Jerusalem might have lived longer, in spite of feudal disorders, if reenforcements had come from home. But Europe allowed the Moslems to recover from their defeat, with the result that Edessa was lost in 1144, and the Christian garrison massacred. When the news reached Europe, the old fires blazed again. Saint Bernard of Clairvaux, cheeks wasted with fasting and eyes glowing with a deep passion for Christ, stepped into the shoes of Peter the Hermit and preached the Second Crusade. France again heard the old battle-cry: "God wills it." Again there was a frantic rush to take the Cross; Bernard and his priests tore up their vestments to fashion crosses of red on the shoulders of the new recruits. Louis VII of France, and Conrad III of Germany went at the head of four hundred thousand men. All they accomplished was another massacre of German Jews. Many Crusaders perished in Asia Minor, and a struggling remnant suffered final defeat at Damascus in 1148. A pitiful handful returned, in perfect disgrace, to their homes.

Then came the most romantic Crusade of them all. In the Third adventure we have the stories of Saladin, brilliant and chivalrous Sultan of Egypt; of Richard "Cœur de Lion" of England, and of Frederick

Barbarossa, called Redbeard, who was the Holy Roman Emperor. Under such auspices it should have been a triumph; it was bitter, galling defeat. Redbeard was drowned in Cilicia after two splendid victories over the Moslems, Richard fell out with Philip Augustus of France, who abruptly returned home, leaving the Lion-Hearted to go on without him. The final outcome was a truce whereby Jerusalem went under the control of the Saladin. It was the old story: frustration, quarreling and defeat.

So they failed; men, soldiers, even the Holy Father were powerless in the face of such disintegrating forces. Peter the Hermit had preached and disappeared; Urban had rallied the faithful only to see them drift into the sands. Saint Bernard was to fan the waning flame, and watch it die. In 1212 a faint shadow of Peter and Bernard arose to preach another Crusade. Stephen of Vendome, a shepherd boy, gathered around him thirty thousand boys and girls, twelve years old and younger, and inflamed them with zeal to take the Holy City where all others had failed. This was the Children's Crusade, the most piteous episode of history. White robes on their shoulders, flickering wax candles in their hands, they sang hymns in a childish treble as they moved toward Marseilles, where, Stephen said, the waters of the ocean would open for them as they had opened at the Red Sea for the children of Israel. They did not seem to understand when the waters did not open; nor when they were tricked aboard ships in the harbor by two slave-dealers. They sailed away singing—to Africa and Egypt and slavery. Two ships were wrecked in a storm, and the sea was white with baby-faces, victims not only of slave-sellers but of superstition and misguided zeal. It was a terrific price, and it purchased nothing.

There were seven major Crusades, not counting the abortive folly of the children. It was a two-hundred-year conflict with Saracen swords, relentless desert sun and internal dissension. Yet the Crusaders have left a deep scar on history's record, and a definite influence on the actions and manners of men who knew nothing whatever of the movement as a whole. Some claim that this influence was totally bad, that the Crusades were too bloody and cruel—which they were. Others declare that they were born in the selfish crafty mind of Urban; doubtless that is true. Some writers have unfairly played up nothing but the gruesome and ugly features and the tragic evil which followed them. They have a case: if we are to be true to historical fact, we must admit that there was much evil in them and out of them. They gave birth to the abuse later known as the sale of indulgences; they separated the Greek Church in the East from the Latin Church in the West; they bred in spirit the Albigensian and Hussite Wars; they heralded by their spirit of intolerance the miserable In-quisition. That is the dark side of the picture.

But is that all? Is the canvas totally black and evil, with no redeeming colors of light? Did nothing good come out of these death-journeys from Paris and Rome and London to Galilee? More good came out of them than most men dream of. For one thing, the Crusades were a counter-offensive against the Turk, which saved Europe from a Moslem invasion when she was least pre-pared to receive it. Powerful rulers like Richard and Barbarossa did not rally to the cause merely to rescue the Holy Sepulcher. They saw in the Turk, advancing on Constantinople, a genuine threat to the peace of the West, and they saw the Moslem armies pouring through that breach across the Bosphorus into Europe. They struck at that menace through Constantinople, and carried the war into the land of the Turk to keep it from their own.

While the movement of the Crusades toward the East took that conflict out of Europe, it also absorbed the hundred and one petty wars that were already there. Petty quarreling was abandoned when the first of the fighting men set their faces toward the rising sun; knights who had once fought each other now stood shoulder to shoulder in a finer cause than they had ever known before. Plunder there was for them, but more hazardous and difficult to secure than that which lay at home. But after criticizing this plunder motive, there remains the fact that the cry, "To arms for the Christ," tore the men of Europe from petty thievery and killing to fight for what, to them at least, was an ideal which lay beyond victory or defeat, even peace with God. Urban may have been dominated by selfishness, but it is too much to suppose that those tens of thousands who perished along the way or on the ramparts of Jerusalem and Antioch were solely selfish in their motives. The fact that the politicians who brought the last Great War down upon our heads were ruled by greed or the lust for power does not affect in the least the motives of the millions who laid down their lives in the firm belief that God was with them in their war to end all war. They may have perished for a profaned hope; so may the Crusader.

West met East, and both were helped. Travel is a great leveler: much of the old animosity of the European for the Oriental evaporated as they came in closer contact. The wondrous arts of the East were carried westward when the Crusaders returned home. Arabic language, science and literature came on a pilgrimage to stand in the schools with the language, science and literature of Europe. Learning was stimulated. In the East were found fine translations of the great philosopher, Aristotle, which largely formed the foundations of thought for Christian scholasticism, so vital in Chris-

tian history.   Above all, the new touch of Greek culture
prepared the way for the coming Renaissance.

In the fighting of the Crusades half the world went
to find out how the other half lived, and came back
with the picture of a different civilization in their minds
as well as less valuable plunder in their saddle-bags.
Farmers and landowners came in contact with Syrian
methods of agriculture with beneficial results: irrigation
was brought to Europe, and everywhere began to appear
strange new crops of hemp, fruits and rice.   Merchants
fingered the delicate cloths of the East, marveled at their
texture and weave, and carried to Europe new luxurious
muslins, damasks and silks.   Commerce and industry
in these and other commodities were enlarged and improved.   Trading cities were revived along the Mediterranean: Barcelona, Genoa and Venice leaped into
wealth and fame.   Navigation was rediscovered, better
ships were built, new trade-lanes in the ocean found
and charted.   The scientist, the sailor and the store-
keeper had new seas to voyage in.   Chemists and medical
men discovered the chemistry and medicines of the
Orient, with the result that Europe decreased its faith
in holy relics and saints' bones, and increased its reliance on pharmacy and surgery.

Larger sympathies were developed not only between
East and West, but also between the nations of Europe.
Frenchman, German and Italian, fighting for the first

time in a common cause, got rid of many petty, sense-
less prejudices, and of many tyrant, feudal rulers.
Feudalism was itself at last trampled to death beneath
the feet of serf, lord and proud prince, as all three
marched to the tune of "God wills it," in the name of
religious faith. Serfs found themselves promoted on
the field of battle, proving themselves often better men
than their "lords." Out of it all arose the "Third
Estate," a powerful, moneyed, middle class. In this
result alone was a transfer of power from brutal baron
to the "little" man: in it, too, are the beginnings of
democracy.

The Crusades, in a feeble, fatal way, satisfied the
spiritual cravings of the age. They enriched and tempered a crude barbaric Europe, and proved that Europe
might be united religiously more than it had ever been
politically. A new drive came to the motive powers of
civilization, a new and broader vision to men. This is
quite clearly seen in Raymond Lull, who went, alone,
in 1291, on another Crusade. He carried no sword in
his hand, no wild schemes of blood and vengeance in
his heart. He went instead to preach, in Arabic, to the
Moslem in North Africa. He was martyred. But before
he died, Lull had established an interest in the teaching of Arabic, Greek, Hebrew and Chaldee in the Universities of the West. He was moreover the first of a
long line of Crusaders who still strive to beat down the

Saracen sword with the love of Jesus Christ. They have built schools and colleges on the very trails the old Crusaders followed. They are slowly convincing the East that the Christ of Peace is the hope of the East. They are more like the original Eleven Crusaders of God, who went out unarmed in obedience to the last command of their Leader: "Go ye, therefore, and teach . . ."

Chapter XI

THE GRAY FRIAR AND THE BLACK

THE Crusaders were resting, one hot day in 1219, when a strange monk walked into their camp. He preached a new kind of sermon, a message that hurt. These Crusaders knew preaching of another sort: the fiery tirades of the monks and bishops who traveled with them, and who bent every effort to fire them with holy zeal for the "cause" by heaping coals of fire upon the heads of the Saracens. But such was not the spiritual stock in trade of this stranger. He heaped his coals upon the heads of the Crusaders themselves, took them to task for their outrages and massacres, condemned the moral corruption of the army, and told them they would surely be defeated unless it stopped. He left them staring, open-mouthed, and went boldly out—toward the camp of the enemy. The fool would be killed!

But he was not killed. He preached to the Sultan on "Peace, and Good-will," and disappeared as quickly as he came. He was Francis of Assisi, the spiritual wonder of the world, a saint and a saintly vagabond. He was the high light of faith in the darkest night of the Church.

He was providentially raised to retouch the fading picture of Christ, making it as lovely in the human sense as in the divine, and giving it back to a forlorn people who had almost given up hope of ever seeing it again.

The world of the thirteenth century needed a man like Francis, for faith and song were almost dead. Who could sing in the midst of constant, devastating war? Who could hope for a better world while staggering beneath the heavy taxes imposed by grasping bishop and sneering king? Who knew where to turn for spiritual comfort when the clergy kept concubines and preached celibacy with their tongues in their cheeks? Who dared even think of salvation with the threat of purgatory and hell hanging over his head like a sword on a thin silk thread? Who wanted to go to church to sit through a dead ritual of magic formulæ? The people were afraid, disheartened, sick, the victims of unworthy men who claimed to be the only "true representatives" of Christ on earth, and holding in their hands the keys to heaven and hell. The really spiritually-minded leaders of the Church stood helpless at this ebbtide of faith and truth, and prayed for a deliverer to come.

He came, not as a cleric, in the robes of priest or monk, not from the throne of a pope or the palace of a prince. He came as history's most humble man, second only to

Jesus in poverty, and, like Jesus, a layman. Francis of Assisi was not a priest, yet he formed one of the mightiest orders of ministers, which fell in line in the wake of the first Eleven. He came to fame and saint-hood as a beggar, and he remains a most convincing proof that any man, who wills it, can live like Jesus Christ. A walking examplar of the Beatitudes, he is a complete and final denial to the old lie that "Chris-tianity is impossible in our kind of world."

Francis was born with a golden spoon in his mouth, the son of a wealthy Italian merchant. For twenty-two years he tried his best to be happy as he squandered his father's gold. He shared in the vices of his day, and became the ringleader of the rich young wasters of Assisi. With them he rode out on a gay feudal war with the neighboring city of Perugia, thinking surely to be back at his winecups and silk clothes within a fortnight. But he was confined for two years a prisoner of war in a Perugian prison, and in that dungeon-darkness his eyes began to open. A desperate sickness overtook him soon after his release, and the pain of it stabbed him fully awake. His extremity was God's opportunity, and he returned to Assisi no longer a gay young blade looking for street-fights and excitement, but a sober youth with a feeling that there was sterner work for him to do, and with a burning eagerness to be at it. He held a final banquet, was properly enthroned as king of the frolic and chief clown, and electrified the feasters by saying good-by to them for ever. He turned with that gesture to embrace "his lady poverty," and to give himself to a life of service to humanity. It is unbelievable that such a man, with so tender a spirit, could be raised in that age. It seeems incredible that this rich young man should one day ride his handsome charger to the bloody slaughter of war, and the next day leap from that charger to kiss the hands of a leper at the side of the road. Few persons in history can rival him; no other faith has ever produced his peer.

He purposely became as poor as Christ and threw aside his royal silks to clothe himself in the tattered rags of a beggar. Purposely! To fight to better advantage the crass materialism which had gripped his world. That was indeed his greatest contribution. He freed men from their passionate love for things and twisted their eyes around that they might look at Christ; he proved to them that there was more genuine joy in a peaceful singing heart than in coffers full of gold. As a rich youth he had been worried, as a beggar he could sing. By embracing poverty he did what the monks, bound as they were to rich abbeys and monasteries, could not do. He stopped many a young feudal war by his simple sincere reflection of the spirit of his Lord, and he set under way a revolution, both social and religious, which made for democracy, social service and a life of vital lay Christianity. Francis changed the slogan of his day from "Every man for himself" to "Sell all that thou hast, and . . . follow me." It was the most far-reaching revolution since Jesus, accomplished without the shedding of a single drop of blood.

He gave faith and hope and the power of religion back to the common people, who needed it most. The poor little man of Assisi threw open the door which all too long had been held shut against their knocking. He convinced the recluse-monks in their retreats that monasticism was not the true Christian form of life, and he threw open the advantages of holy living to every one without the acceptance of monastic vows. In other words, he made God accessible again to common men. He taught them that the only condition of salvation was repentance, turning back to God, and living at peace with one another. He shot society through with humility, peace, mutual helpfulness and pacifism. He saved Christianity in the thirteenth century for all centuries thereafter.

"He gave the world a cry of pain turned into song," wrote some one. He started a vibrant singing joy in life and the world, making men forget their fear of a universe they could not understand in the thought that God made it and therefore it was to be enjoyed. He loved the materials of God without ever becoming a materialist. He sang songs to the wind and the rain, to leaves on the trees and rocks on the mountainside. To him it was "Brother Sun" and "Sister Wind." He preached to the birds, called out gladly to fierce "Brother Wolf" in the forest. He gave glad utterance to fresh and wholesome ideas of nature and human life and religion, which were the dawn of a new era. Religiously, the Saint was the forerunner of the Reformation; in his zest for humanity he was the road-builder of the Renaissance.

Francis was no scholar; he read men instead of books. He rather feared learning and the long studies of the schoolmen because he felt they would put his friars out of touch with the real needs of the unlettered world. Yet his influence on literature was great. His "Song to Brother Sun" became an epic, and it marks the beginning of national literature in Europe. He started all Italy singing his rollicking hymns in the vernacular Italian. Little did he know that he was clearing the way for Dante, who was to write the *Divine Comedy* in the "vulgar tongue." Dante, immortal as his epic, is better known than Francis to students of literature, yet in his passion for this world and in his use of the new language he was merely picking up the tool dropped by Francis when he reached out his emaciated arms to welcome "Sister Death."

He died in 1226, only forty-four years old, nearly

blind from excessive weeping. The world scarcely knew
how to live without him. Men everywhere called him
the replica of Jesus, and said he had upon him the very
"stigmata" of the Christ, the prints of the nails on
hands and feet. However that may have been, he
surely had in his heart the stigmata of the spirit, and in
the shedding of that spirit he became and remains the
big brother of humanity, the bringer of more hope and
faith and love than ever came through any other man
save Christ himself. He left behind him a streak of
clear white light in an age of dirt and darkness. He
left behind him as well the "Order of Saint Francis," a
multitude of missionary brothers inspired with purpose-
ful poverty and robed in gray. They are the Gray
Friars, whose record of honorable missionary endeavor
is, next to his own spirit, his most enduring monument.

A different order was established by Dominic the
Spaniard, whose approach was less democratic, and
whose followers were to be known as the Black Friars.
Both orders were impelled by the passionate purpose to
keep God vital in the lives of men, though they came
at their problem from different directions, across different avenues of approach. Francis warmed the heart,
and Dominic quickened the mind. The first was a
devotional leader who moved in the realm of the emo-
tions, the second a teacher who followed the labyrin-
thine passages of the intellect. Where the man from

Assisi sought to strengthen faith by striking at materialism, the man from Spain tried to keep it and the Church pure and undefiled by striking at heresy. He sent forth his Friars to search out those who had lapsed into unbelief and doubt. Some wandered over into the lands of the Mohammedan and the Japanese, who had never heard of Jesus Christ, but most of them labored with those of their own kind who had heard and forgotten. They were good and sincere men, able teachers whose weapons were reason, argument, debate and explanation. But they had the two cardinal limitations of most teachers: they were often narrow-minded and half-informed. Blazing with enthusiasm for their gleams of holy truth, they forgot that other men might have *other* gleams. In their zeal to make men think their way they committed the regrettable mistake of acting as judges and torturers for the Inquisition. Their black mantles were blended into the somber shadows of torture-room and dungeon, and much of their good work was lost in a welter in innocent blood.

The Inquisition is a dark blot on the escutcheon of the Church. There was no excuse for it, though it is all quite easily understood when we consider the medieval mind. Heresy was regarded as a deadly poison in the blood-stream of the Church, threatening her life and power. And the Dominican was determined to purge the Church of that poison. The Inquisition failed.

Inquisitions always fail. Intolerance and persecution
are the poorest of weapons. Real truth is born not out
of stubborn allegiance to a single grain of it, but from
the free exchange of opinions, ideas and revelations.
The greatest of sins in the Christian may be the sin of
the closed mind, the calloused heart and power misap-
plied. Heresy is not so much a disease as it is the symp-
tom of a disease.

Yet, when all is said, it is unfair to remember these
teachers under Dominic the Spaniard for nothing but
the heartless Inquisition. They have a long and honorable record of service. They rivaled the Franciscan,
more than once, in errands of charity and relief. When
the Black Death swept Europe, the Black Friars showed
their mettle by going into sick-rooms in the face of
certain death, by gathering and burying the dead while
other men quailed behind locked doors. Heroic as that
was, it appears to be insignificant when compared with
the work they did in making Christianity intellectually
respectable.

One's blood tingles as one reads of the work of
Dominican scholars. Think of Friar Roger Bacon, who
laid the foundations of modern science and the ex-
perimental method. He studied everything from Hebrew to optics, and demonstrated an encyclopedic
knowledge in his work *Opus Majus*. From within the
shadows of the Church he was the first modern to

emphasize the difference between the theories of theologians who would be scientists, and the facts proved by the experiments of men who *were* scientists. He sent men back to unlock the secrets of nature by studying it at first hand, and he was the father of modern inductive reasoning. A brave and persecuted soul, held even to be in league with the devil, Friar Bacon opened a new world when he induced men to tear themselves free from superstition and magic, and to ascend to the higher levels of true knowledge and culture.

Other scholars were busy in the important task of reconciling the longings and aspirations of the heart with the keen logic of the brain. Peter Lombard wrote on *God, Man, Salvation, Sacraments and Last Things,* and so completely met the needs of his age that he remained unchallenged for two centuries. Thomas Aquinas, a Dominican, set the theological standards of the Roman Church. One of his statements sounds remarkably modern: "Religion is rational and reason is divine; all knowledge and all truth must be capable of harmonious adjustment." Duns Scotus, a Franciscan, took issue with Aquinas in discounting the rational basis of faith and insisted that theology should be separated from philosophy. John Wyclif was another of the great scholastics who is especially remembered by his English translation of the Bible and by leading a revolt against papal aggressions and corruptions in England.

It is interesting to note that Wyclif, Huss and Luther, the great reformers, were all university professors. Two others must be mentioned because their work shook the old foundations of ignorance to their lowest stones. Anselm was orthodox, a loyal son of the Church, an able defender of her doctrines, and best remembered by his notable book on the Atonement. His attitude may be expressed in his words: "I believe that I may understand." Abelard objected to that, took an opposite view and said, "I understand that I may believe." Abelard's fearless espousal of reason as the partner of faith opened the door into religious freedom, but his voice was promptly stilled by the narrower ecclesiastics.

The scholastics of this medieval age doubtless quibbled over what to us would seem trifles. They argued, for instance, as to "how many angels could dance on the point of a needle." But lest we laugh too soon, let us remember that all knowledge has had humble beginnings, and that learning has moved up slowly out of misconception and misguidance into truth in its greater fullness. It is right to point out the intellectual errors or bigotry of early Christian thought, but we do well to remember that all other thought has had the same evolution. Was not chemistry once alchemy? Does not the history of medicine have a large place for quackery? Was not astronomy born out of the random guesses of astrology? Those old debates were the first shots fired in the greatest upheaval of all times, and they were the beginning of the battle to free the mind of man. The men who took part in those conflicts brought about a greater freedom than did the men who freed the slaves of Athens and Rome.

We are the heirs of Abelard, we who believe because we understand. We live in a world or rather a universe of which Abelard in his wildest moments never even dreamed. We look out into millions of miles of space, and discover that we are pigmies on a flying island in the sky. Our scientists look through their tubes of glass to find mountains on the moon, double stars, comets and meteors. Others have found the atom and the electron to be the basic, secret units of life. Out of the blinding speed of the stars and the bewildering complexities of the atom have come to us a new sense of the largeness and greatness of God. It is a larger world, a supremely powerful Creator. We look, and study, and understand: and because we understand we believe. Abelard and Aquinas started *that*. It is true that the Church has at times opposed the march of science and knowledge; it is also true that the modern spirit of free investigation and experiment began in these early men of the Church, who rattled their chains of mental bondage in the medieval night and cried like Jacob to the angels of darkness: "Let me go, for the day breaketh."

Everywhere, then, under the influence of these

questioning minds, knowledge began to grow and glow. Men began to ask, "Why—How—When?" Everywhere the monastic schools of yesterday were growing, enlarging, stretching themselves up toward the stature of full-fledged universities. Among the earliest were Paris, teaching theology, where Abelard and Dante and Loyola burned their midnight oil; Oxford, Alma Mater of England's great; Bologna in Italy, famous for law, and Italian Salerno, specializing in medicine. The Franciscans and Dominicans moved in upon these universities, and captured them. For centuries the only genuine scholars and teachers in the Western World were Christian. Christianity gripped and held the mind of Europe; and the teachers of the Church shaped the thought of Western civilization.

The Gray Friars and their brothers in Black had their day of power, and gave way to the Jesuits. The universities where they worked have evolved into the modern school of higher learning. Harvard, Yale and Princeton are the direct descendants of Paris, Oxford, Bologna and Salerno, dependent upon them for their general schemes of organization, their systems of examinations and degrees. Through the portals of these modern schools comes yearly a flood of youth, having upon them the stigmata of Francis and of Dominic. They are doctors, ministers, social workers, thinking more of service than of money; they are engineers, chemists, teachers, research workers in a thousand fields, who have found God in their test-tubes, who have reconciled faith and learning, who as the heirs of the first Christian schoolmen have firmly fixed in them the ideal that only he who searches for the truth and finds it, shall be free.

CHAPTER XII

THE BREAKING POINT

THE Middle Ages, like all other ages, waned and died. Medievalism had to reach its peak and go down the other side of Time's hill. There had to come, in short, a breaking point between the ages, a crossing of the line dividing that which was old and outworn from that which was new and necessary. There was no sharp or sudden breaking, no quick crossing of the line, but rather a merging of the medieval into the modern. Some sailed across the line slowly, in ships. Marco Polo journeyed to unexplored lands in the East, to become the first globe trotter and a guest in the palace of the Great Khan of China. The Portuguese sailed around Cape Verde, Christopher Columbus walked the deck of the *Santa Maria*, looking for a short way to India and finding a new world. Vasco da Gama reached India, and Magellan circumnavigated the earth, Balboa crossed the Isthmus of Panama and climbed a high hill to be the first white man to look on the Pacific. Cortez conquered the Aztec in Mexico, and Pizarro took Peru. At the mastheads of the discoverers, out ahead of the armies of the conquerors, rode the banner of the Cross.

While the soldier with his musket was blowing open a path into a new world, the priest who went with him, with his baptismal water and crucifix, was laying the first foundations of order and civilization.

But we are ahead of our story. Long before Columbus paced the deck of his caravel and Magellan gave his name to the "Straits," men were busy everywhere fighting their way across the line. Some stabbed their way with a pen, that weapon more powerful than the sword. Some leaped over into the new age with the brushes of the artist in their hands; others were sculptors, as with mallet and chisel, they hewed out the first rough outlines of a new art. We call them the men of the "Renaissance," or the "rebirth." This revival was a glorious outburst of enthusiasm in human life, art, literature, learning and the sciences. It was the breaking point of the ages, the turning point of history.

Petrarch, a knight of the pen, may well be called the first leader of the Renaissance. He uttered its battle-cry and the challenge, that: "Every man has a right to his own opinion, *this life has a value of its own.*" He was the pioneer "Humanist." Men everywhere snatched at his cry, as thirsty travelers, after long wandering in the desert, grasp a drink of water. They were so tired of the endless bickering of the scholars, so weary with the old theological disputes which seemed to them to have no connection whatever with life. They had been tortured too long with vague threats of hell and purgatory, while this life, about whose reality alone they were sure, slipped away from them. And here was Petrarch, talking like Saint Francis, writing of love and nature and the sun. He made life seem good, he robbed men of much of their superstitious fear, and made their lives glow with happiness.

His disciple and friend Boccaccio, the story-teller, was as much alive as Petrarch. He went further in singing of the lusty joys of life. His stories, in their effort to be human, became lewd, coarse and crude, so that even to-day, sophisticated and experienced as we are, we hesitate to put his *Decameron* into the hands of untutored youth. These two wrote in the "vulgar" tongue of Dante, and the work of Boccaccio was indeed vulgar in more ways than one, and it illustrates the pernicious effects of the Renaissance.

Paganism in its evil forms as well as its good reentered Europe during this rebirth of art. The old pagan culture was revived in all its glory; exquisite vases were dug from the ruins of old cities, priceless sculptures were found and restored and exhibited for public admiration. The old Greek and Latin masterpieces of literature were circulated by the thousand; Virgil became a god of letters, Cicero a resurrected saint. Out of the East, as Constantinople fell, came a horde of Greek scholars bringing to Europe new translations of

Plato, Homer and Aristotle. These men threw open a window to the past as well as to the future, making all other men the heirs of all the lost beauty of the ages. This period of rebirth was truly a golden hour, but it was not enough. It ran away with the men who lived in it, making them forgetful of the very things they most needed. Struggling nobly for the prizes of earth, they forgot to seek the prizes of life.

Machiavelli, for instance, was the typical product of the Italian Renaissance. This pagan and cynic represented everything in politics and government that was outrageously unethical and treacherous. He devised a system of lawlessness, falsehood and ruthlessness under the guise of freedom. He was the most striking example of his day that men care more for license than for liberty. Most men go drunk and cruel when too much freedom is placed quickly in their hands. It was so with Machiavelli, who became as intolerant toward religion as religion had once been toward art. He "acted the snob, and failed as a candidate for individual fame."

Brightest star in the Renaissance firmament was Lorenzo the Magnificent, a Florentine and a Medici, one of a family of bloody power, infamous cardinals and popes which reached its climax in Catharine. Lorenzo, as head of the Florentine Republic, was profusely generous with his money as a patron of the arts and sciences and literature. Achieving some reputation as an author

and artist himself, he wrote a famous play on Julian the
Apostate, putting into the mouth of this pagan Roman
Emperor the words, "Thou hast conquered, O pale Galilean." That line was not merely a figure of speech but
a bitter cry wrung from the heart of Lorenzo himself,
a confession that the supreme expression of beauty had
not been delivered by the emancipated of the awakening. To be complete, the Renaissance had to become
Christian, Aristotle had to meet Christ, the courage of
the Greek had to be blended with the beauty of Jesus.

Such a blending had already started, before the days
of Petrarch, with the cathedral-builders. Whole communities gathered, trade guilds were organized, to put
their dreams and hopes in solid visible form through the
medium of the Gothic cathedrals. In place of the old
Basilica and Romanesque churches, which at best looked
like grim repellent fortresses, the new cathedrals were
prayers in stone which held beauty and stateliness.
Their high pointed arches and soaring roofs have lifted
generations of men out of the mire of the commonplace
and have sent their souls singing up to God. Their
stained-glass windows, centuries old, have let through
a hallowed mellow light into the heart of many an earth-
wearied man. "It was a long cry," says Doctor Monsma
in his recent *Story of the Church,* "from the cave-man
huts of the old European barbarians to the mighty
arches of Gothic architecture, from the shrill war

whoops of Attila's Huns to the 'for ever and ever' of
the silent cathedral vastnesses." Mankind was on the
march, and their marching was made easier, more lovely,
by the spirit of the Eleven who went ahead.

The Christian artists came into these cathedrals and
churches to decorate the walls and ceilings and to call
back art to a nobler ideal. With the pagan it had been
"art of art's sake;" with the Christian it was "art for
Christ's sake." Henceforth art was to serve as a medium
in translating ideals and aspirations that lay beyond
anything merely human. Into it also came a new face,
that of the Madonna, whose advent meant a new epoch
in painting. The old barbarians had no use for that
face; the finest of the new artists now placed it in the
center of their canvases. Raphael joined the immortals
as his holy brush brought into being *The Sistine Madonna,* in which the spirit of Saint Francis seems hover-
ing over his hand while he united Christian ideals with
the amazingly human forms of his subjects. Giotto
painted in another studio, telling his legends of the saints
in terms of stark human drama. Who can ever tell
worthily the story of Michelangelo, the creator of
David and *The Last Judgment?* "His statue of Bacchus,"
says Raphael, "rivals anything ever done by Phidias or
Praxitiles." Time has produced no more inspired or
versatile hand than Angelo's, nor has any other man been
more influential in art.

The greatest of them all was Leonardo da Vinci. School children to-day know the characters of his *Last Supper,* and the smile of his *Mona Lisa* is familiar to all who know pictures at all. He was the most complete and versatile man in the Renaissance world, and few excel him in any other period. He was an engineer, a musician, a painter, a sculptor, a poet, and a philosopher. Historians rate him as one of the real pioneers of science, hold him famous for his work on capillary attraction and flying machines! He was so strong that he could break a horseshoe with his fingers, yet he was known often to buy caged birds in order to set them free. Strength, coupled with kindness, made this universal genius the perfect example of the influence of Christianity on the pagan foundations of art.

All this rebirth in art took place in Italy and the South. North of the Alps the awakening took a different turn. There the motive and influence were religious, concerned as much with the Scriptures and spirituality as with culture and the classics. The leading rôle of the northern revival was played by a wit who had the soul of a saint. Erasmus was a Hollander, long-nosed, timid, nervous, a humorist, who was also the first man to make his living solely by writing books. Like most humorists, Erasmus was one of the saddest of men. He was kicked about like a human football from the cradle to the grave. Born out of wedlock, he was hustled into a cloister and into the ranks of the clergy against his will. Still he smiled, and in course of time he wrote *The Praise of Folly*, parading in that book, to the tune of bitter sarcasm and biting wit, the super- stitions and hair-splitting arguments of the scholars. But Erasmus, laugh-merchant though he was, knew what he was about. Beneath the thin veneer of humor there lay a burning conviction that there was some- thing rotten in the state of the Church, something shameful in the way religion was being represented to the common man. He challenged the groundless authority of the priests, stood forth as champion for their victims. "May not a man be a Christian," he asked, "who can not explain philosophically how the nativity of The Son differs from the procession of the Holy Spirit? The sum of religion is peace, which can only be when definitions are as few as possible and opinion is left free on many subjects." Erasmus was a good friend of the individual, and crier of a new day when each man would be his own priest and each true worshiper would carry an altar of his own in his heart.

Erasmus did more than this. He published an edi- tion of the Greek New Testament, with a new Latin translation, and put his work within reach of the peo- ple. In this precious volume men discovered the truths long kept from them and decided that the old authority

which had bound them was neither true nor just. Then
Erasmus died, of a broken heart, hated by reformers and
unreformed alike, without confession or absolution,
gasping pitifully with his last breath, *"Lieber Gott."*
His work however was well done: he had helped men
to think for themselves. After the great Reformation
had got under way, men began saying that "Erasmus
laid the egg and Luther hatched it."

Erasmus wanted reform, but not revolution. He was
afraid of that, and he hated it as relentlessly as he hated
war. He tried his best to reform the Church from
within, but he proved to be a King Canute of the mind,
unable to stem the tides of open rebellion. The tides
had been gathering force too long to be stopped now.
A hundred years before Erasmus, John Wyclif had tried
the same method of "boring from within." Wyclif,
known to fame as "the morning star of the Reformation," was professor, teacher, patriot, champion of freedom. He stirred up a Peasant's Revolt, created an order
of lay preachers and put into the hands of the Englishman the first Bible written in *English,* which was as
important an event as the invention of the steam engine
or the flying of Franklin's kite. Wyclif's Bible worked
miracles in a day when grammar, dictionary and
spelling-book were unknown; it did more than any
other single book to fix the standards of the English
language. That was the contribution of keen-eyed,

gray-bearded John Wyclif, who lived in a hovel as lowly
and poor as a certain stable in Bethlehem.

That Bible might have been used to good advantage,
but there were too many Belshazzars in the councils of
the Church who could not read the handwriting of
Wyclif and Erasmus.   These blind ones called the
English Bible "the work of the devil," and did their
best to seize and burn every copy in the land.   Did they
succeed?   Did any man ever succeed in setting himself
against the march of truth?   How far they succeeded
we well know.

Selfridge, the great London department store, in the
year 1931, sent in an order to William Collins and Sons,
publishers, for one hundred thousand copies of a new
edition of the Holy Bible!   That is probably the largest
single order ever placed for any book.   Said the store
managers: "There is only one Book of which any business
firm would dare to order one hundred thousand
copies."   Thanks to John Wyclif, we have a Bible in
nearly every language that men speak!   Thanks to
John Wyclif, the best news on earth is still the good
news of Christ!

Wyclif died in bed.   Unusual, that.   Thirty years
later the Council of Constance dug up his body, burned
it and threw his ashes into a tiny brook that runs past
Lutterworth into the Avon.   A prophet of the day
wrote a verse on the infamous deed:

> "The Avon to the Severn runs,
>   The Severn to the sea;
> And Wyclif's dust shall spread abroad
>   Wide as the waters be."

The prophet was right. The waters were wide. Before that same Council of Constance stood John Huss of Bohemia, disciple of Wyclif, lover even of his ashes. Huss fought a brave fight for freedom—and Bohemia. He stirred up a bloody national war and a whole series of Hussite wars. He did not die in bed. The Council burned him at the stake, and his ashes blew from the stake into the sea to float on the tides for ever with the ashes of the Englishman. Did we say once that Paul made Jesus international? Do you doubt it? We present as witnesses Erasmus the Hollander, Huss the Bohemian, Savonarola the Florentine, Luther the German.

Savonarola? He was the last to be burned. A firebrand like Stephen, he lacked the mental balance of the first reformers, yet he was so dangerous to truth that he had to be burned. Luther? He was the son of a German miner, fifteen years old when the sky caught the ruddy glow from the stake in Florence as Savonarola died. He nailed a public notice to the door of an obscure German church on Hallowe'en, and the pounding of his hammer shook the earth.

CHAPTER XIII

REBELLION AND REFORMATION

MARTIN LUTHER and his memory are filled with glory and contradictions. He was the titan of heroes, the humblest of men. He was brutally coarse and kindly to a fault, a driving despot and a loving husband, a mystic and a dealer in practicalities. He was an Augustinian monk and jolly, terribly in earnest about God and men, yet filled with laughter and the Hallowe'en spirit. The Hallowe'en adventure he had on All Saints Eve of 1517, he never thought of as an adventure at all. Neither was there any idea whatever in his mind that what he was doing would be of as great concern to posterity as the signing of Magna Charta or the crowning of Charlemagne. He scarcely realized that the sheets of paper he carried in his hand that Hallowe'en concealed so much dynamite. When it exploded, Martin Luther himself was the most surprised man on earth. He is, by accident, the demigod of heroism.

Luther was not even in the Hallowe'en mood that night. He was mad at Tetzel, at the Pope and at the Roman Catholic Church. He was mad, as Jesus and

Saint Paul and Saint Francis had been mad, at oppression and deceit and heartless lust for gold. He was mad at strong men who were putting spiritual blinders on the weak. The accumulated anger of the age was boiling in the merry monk's blood. The intellectual, political and economic injustices that marked his day were coming to a head, a breaking-point, in him.

Luther turned first upon Tetzel, a Dominican by choice or calling, a salesman of the "go-getter" school by inclination. He was sent out by Pope Leo X to raise money, on a commission basis, for the building of Saint Peter's Cathedral at Rome. It was a good choice: salesman-Tetzel had lungs of leather, the craft of the fox and a commodity to sell which needed little bally-hoo. He peddled "indulgences." An indulgence was a short way of buying an entrance into heaven. It was a convenience whereby a sinner might gain forgiveness for his sins, or for the sins of a dead friend in purgatory, by a cash contribution to the building program of the Pope. Inasmuch as all men living were surely sinners and all men dead were presumably in purgatory, Tetzel had a wide field. Cheap, quick salvation! Men leaped at it. They left their parish priests, turned their backs on the sacraments, as Tetzel beckoned merrily for them to come and buy on his easy plan. Shaking his money-box under their noses, he cried: "Drop a penny in my box for some poor wretch in purgatory and the moment

it clinks on the bottom, the freed soul flies up to heaven."
He promised remission for the sins of yesterday, for the
sins of the hour just gone by, even for sins that might
be committed to-morrow or next year. It was the
crowning insult, the final offense to decency and faith.
Luther, then a professor in the University of Wittenberg, watching the cheap fraud, resolved to stop it.
"I'll beat a hole in his drum," said Luther. But he did
vastly more than that. He wrecked Tetzel's drum, and
set up a drum-music of his own. A wild, free, con-
tagious music which came to be the prelude of the rolling of the drums of modern liberty. Luther stepped
into line behind that one who died on a Cross to set
men free; he took his cadence and his beat from Eleven
Drummers out of Galilee whose beats were shortly to
become the heart-beats of humanity.

Luther's fierce music was written not in staffs or
measures, but in the form of ninety-five "theses" against
indulgences, ninety-five reasons why they were a mis-
chief and an evil. He closed his arguments with an open
challenge to a debate on the whole subject. Then he
strode down the street to the town church, and nailed
his arguments and his challenge to its great oak door.
There was nothing unusual in that. The door was the
village bulletin board, and other professors had nailed
other notices there which the people stopped to read,
half-understanding and half-interested. But when they

read the notice of Professor Luther, they understood, and they were more than half-interested. All Germany had been waiting for a notice like that. It was not merely a formal challenge to a usual debate, but a daring defiance to the crushing power of Rome. Between the lines they read of an amazingly brave attack on institutional privilege in the name of human, individual rights. It was a declaration of war, the spring-board of the Protestant Reformation.

Luther got the debate he had asked for. Tetzel scurried away with his money-box under his arm, frightened out of his pardon-selling and out of his wits by the roar which greeted the notice on the Wittenberg door. The Pope himself took a hand and sent down his best debaters to put Luther in his place. Cajetan came, a cardinal: smooth, subtle and Italian; but for all that he blundered. Doctor Luther got the best of him, and Wittenberg and Germany cheered again. Next came a better one, the German Miltitz, who won a temporary truce by making Luther compromise. Then came the third, the famous Doctor Eck, who destroyed the effects of the compromise and made Luther draw his sword again, and engage Eck in a debate, with a flower in his hand. What a touch! Freshness, new beauty, the spring-time hopes of men were on the side of Luther as he shouted: "The just shall live by faith." Tradition, cruel privilege, staleness, the memory of many a bitter winter of the soul were with Eck, who defended the sacraments and "works" of the Church as the sure way to salvation. The swords flashed long between them; they fenced for days and left the field with each side claiming the victory. Pope Leo, watching nervously, trying to fathom Luther, to estimate the force of this tidal-wave of rebellion rising in Germany, resolved on a bold measure. He issued a bull declaring Luther a heretic, threatening excommunication unless he recanted, ordering his writings burned and commanding him to come to Rome within sixty days. It was the crisis, the testing hour. Had Luther gone humbly to the Pope, the rebellion would have died, the Reformation might never have been. *But Luther did not go.* Backed politically by the powerful Elector of Saxony, he taught the Pope a lesson in boldness. He tore the bull to shreds, and hurled it into a public bonfire while his students, townsmen and countrymen went wild with joy. The die was cast. Doctor Luther would stand, alone if need be, against the world.

Now politics entered the play. Charles V, Emperor of Germany, had been watching the fight, wondering what the effect of it would be on his relations with Leo. He summoned Luther to appear and defend himself before a diet, or convocation, at Worms. This time Luther decided to go, in spite of the warnings of his friends that he would be trapped and murdered. Remember, Huss and Savonarola had been burned not long ago. But he went: "Though there were as many devils in Worms as tiles on the house roofs to prevent him," as he wrote to his friend Spalatin. He rode into the city in the cold gray dawn of the most electric day in history. As the rooftops with their tiles came into sight, he rose to his feet and with his rude wagon rocking him from side to side, he roared out the lines of his own hymn:

> "A mighty fortress is our God,
> A bulwark never failing——"

Crowds surged about him, men and women lined the housetops and leaned from windows to shout their sympathy to him. A priest of Rome held up to him a picture of Savonarola, and begged him not to recant. He had a spell of sickness the next day, but at sunset he stood before the diet.

What a spectacle! Martin Luther, peasant son of a humble German miner, alone against—*Rome*. A "heckled monk in a brilliant court." Princes were there, rulers, electors, noblemen, soldiers, statesmen. The Emperor himself presided. Red-capped cardinals from Spain and France sat on a dais and looked at him scornfully as he came through the door. Bishops in robes of violet whispered to one another as he stood quietly, waiting for the blow to fall. It was one strong man against many, a peasant against his king, a rebel-priest against his pope. It was the bid of fluttering freedom against entrenched privilege, liberty against authority, sinister institution against serious individual. It was the hour when liberty came into her own, and democracy was born.

They asked him to recant and confess that he was wrong. They tried their best to make him say that the sacraments of the Church were of greater value than the altars of the individual heart. They worked furiously to make him recall his statement that the Bible was supreme in matters of faith and action. But Luther held his ground, and threw back at them those words which have since become the justification of all honest rebellion: "Here I stand; I can not do otherwise; so help me God." The Spaniards hissed, the Emperor was dumfounded, the faces of the bishops turned as violet as their robes. But the Germans in the diet clapped their hands. He, they, had won. When Luther walked out of that council-chamber, he carried with him as a present for the generations yet unborn the right of every individual to make of his faith a spiritual adventure and not a dumb bowing to the past. No institution, organization, or rite could hereafter stand between a worshiper and his God. Every man was to be his own priest, his own prophet, his own king.

His own king! Men have missed that thought too much. They are too apt to consider the Reformation which followed the diet as a purely religious movement in effect. As a matter of fact, Luther was striking as much at Emperor Charles as he was at Pope Leo. When he stood at Worms to deny the supreme authority and "divine right" of the Pope, he set in motion a series of forces and movements which in time brought about a complete recasting and realignment of human society. In place of the old Roman ideal of "the good of the few at the expense of the many" came the democratic, Christian ideal of "the highest good for the greatest number." That doctrine, Reformation-born, is the chief characteristic of our modern civilization, and it is undeniably the gift of the Christian faith. It has proved to be dangerous doctrine. It swept Louis Capet from the throne of France and sent after him to the guillotine his tragic, beauteous, short-sighted queen, Marie Antoinette. It sent Charles Stuart to the scaffold in England and gave birth to the Puritan Revolution and the English Parliament. It was the driving power of the American colonist, the real occasion for the American Revolution. "Liberty, equality and fraternity," and, "No taxation without representation," slogans of our greatest Revolutions, were new expressions of the old Reformation principle that all authority, religious, political or any other, exists only with the consent of the governed. The battle roars of those revolutions were echoes of the fighting at Worms; political liberty, in its thousand varieties, is the child of the religious liberty gained that day.

While the Reformation resulted in self-governing states, and developed a certain degree of territorial toleration and integrity, it can not be said that it accomplished any great immediate change in the behavior of the nations toward each other. International rivalries went on as before, and continue to our own day. Machiavelli and not Jesus remained the patron saint of statesmanship and diplomacy. Yet Luther dropped one seed that took root quickly. Before the century was out came Hugo Grotius, Christian jurist, arch enemy of war, and father of international law! He loved his own and all other countries equally well, but a little less than he loved one other. Asked what he thought of France, he replied: "France is the most beautiful kingdom there is—after the Kingdom of Heaven." He actually started to show men that the kingdoms of earth could be modeled on this kingdom of heaven, he was the first to teach us to base the law of nations on the Golden Rule. We have been slow to learn that lesson, nor do we bow the knee to Hugo Grotius as we do to the heroes of war. Yet he did not fail. Our twentieth-century "freedom of the seas," our efforts to frame international codes of honor on treatment of wounded and prisoners of war, the extension of arbitration, abolition of privateering of non-belligerents, our lame and halting attempts to humanize war—these are precious endowments created for us by Grotius, through Luther.

When Luther left Worms, he was "kidnaped" by his friends and hurried off to the secret mountainous castle of the Wartburg. Their purpose was to save him from the vengeance of his enemies, but they also gave him the opportunity to forge and fire his second thunderbolt. This was a new translation of the New Testament written not in dead Latin but in living German. What Wyclif had done for the Englishman, what Francis and Dante had done for the Italian, the Rebel of Wittenberg now did for the German. He put into the hands of the people a Testament, and later a whole Bible, written in an idiomatic German they could actually read! He went further and became the creator of "High German," fixing the character of modern German speech. The tongue spoken in modern Germany is the "vulgar" tongue in which Luther wrote his Bible and his hymns. He introduced woodcuts in book form, that those who could not read might see his message in pictures. Before he died all Germany was singing his hymns, repeating in church his perfected German liturgies, studying and memorizing his two Catechisms. Out of this stimulus to national language and literature came an impulse to national education. Schools were founded in increasing numbers by Luther and the reformers who followed him. Monasteries were dissolved and their wealth and revenue turned over to the universities, into which were to come more laymen than priests, with their new Bibles in their hands, and a whole new universe of truth opening up before their questioning eyes. It is all very well to say that Luther "only put an infallible Book in the place of an infallible Church;" let it also be remembered that in throwing open the doors to individual exploration and education he provided the means of a developing freedom and a lessening sense of infallibility.

The rebel married. Luther, ex-monk, married Catherine von Bora, ex-nun. "He has repudiated his vows," cried the Catholics. They both had done so. But in truth they renounced a lesser for the sake of a greater vow, and together they dealt a mortal blow to the double standards of medieval piety. Celibacy, horribly abused, lost its glamour for the true believer, and the marriage of man to woman took on a halo of higher virtue. The married state, indeed, became far more virtuous than the state of celibacy. This marriage of Luther and Catherine not only brought about a house-cleaning in the Roman Church, but it cast a new gleam of sacredness over every domestic fireside in Europe. These two reformers have sent down a vastly ennobling influence to your home and mine. They identified faith with common life and aspirations, religion with household duties. Luther the husband wrote: "It looks like a great thing when a monk renounces everything and goes into a cloister and carries on a life of asceticism. On the other hand it looks like a small thing when a maid cooks and cleans and does other housework. But because God's command is there, even such a small work must be praised as a service of God far surpassing the holiness and asceticism of all monks and nuns." They were happy, these two, and refreshingly human. "What care I if I am in debt?" asks jolly Luther. "Katie pays the bills!"

For twenty-two years they shared life. New conquests came, and then troubles, disappointments, divisions. Scholars deserted him as the once magnificent mind narrowed down and became increasingly conservative. The common people, the peasants, turned against him when, in their Peasants' Revolt, he turned fiercely on them and advised the ruling princes to "knock down, strangle and stab" the "murderous, thieving rabble" into submission. That outburst was typical of Luther, who was so intent on a religious reformation that he did not want it entangled with social revolt. Other reformers crowded him out of glory's spotlight, and took the play from him as old age came nearer. He went home to Eisleben, in 1546, to rest. And there, in the haunts of his childhood, he died.

A merry massive cog in the wheel of God, was Martin Luther. We defy any man to "analyze" him. He was all things to all men. Brilliant and narrow-minded, he left behind him a Reformation which was also brilliant and narrow, constructive and destructive. We regret the lack of tolerance in it, and in its promoters and aftermath. It failed in this and many other aspects because it could not rise above the mean level of its average mind. Its wild and sudden freedom gave birth indirectly to a perfect scourge of wars: the Peasants' Revolt in Germany, the Dutch Revolt in the Netherlands, the Thirty Years' War, the upheavals in France and England and later in America. These were sad inevitable results; but there has never been a revolution without a Terror. The Reformation remains, after all, the most constructive movement of history. It made the Bible supreme on the Bible's own ground, and brought in the first appreciation of a historical sense in the study of it. It rediscovered the supremacy of individual faith and set individual conscience free. It restated the Pauline message of "Justification, forgiveness, by faith," and it turned man's outraged trust from erring pope to loving God. It made Christianity more than ever an adventure in liberty, and called it back to power as the great leavening influence of Western civilization. It gave to subsequent human development and progress a tone more than ever Christian.

CHAPTER XIV

DISSENT AND THE PURITAN STRAIN

SIXTEENTH-CENTURY soil was full of dragon's teeth. Revolt seemed to grow out of the earth, rebellion and revolution were the order of the day. Some came as repercussions of the crashing thunderbolts of Martin Luther, with leaders emboldened by his example. Others were entirely independent of the German movement, rolling up as inevitably as the waves of the sea, the natural breaking of long pent-up forces and undercurrents of the times. Little Switzerland, land of William Tell and Arnold Winkelried, had such an independent revolt, led by a fiery young priest who proved to be a sixteenth-century Stephen. Huldreich Zwingli had the blood and headlong courage of a natural-born rebel. He sowed the wind, reaped the whirlwind and lay dead at forty-seven on a bloody battle-field. Father of the Reformed Church, humanist, critic and lover of men, Zwingli sent toward us two deep streams of influence. He reduced the sacraments to two, Baptism and the Lord's Supper, thus removing much of the old "mystical" tendencies of the old Roman rituals; and he stood for a "puritanical" regulation of life. Puritan! It

is a new word, an octopus of a word, with its timeless
tentacles buried deep in our living, and with few of us
knowing it.   It is a restless, disturbing, exploding word
that has disrupted old empires and built new ones.   Puritan Zwingli upset his nation with it, and when he died
in 1531 he left Switzerland in an uproar, torn by armed
warfare between Catholics and Protestants.   Geneva was
the most turbulent city of the land, caught between the
fire of Catholic bishops and refugee French reformers.   It
was moreover a trade center on the overland route between France and Italy, half-way house of refuge for
the exiled and oppressed.   Geneva became a Babel
of opinions, and, according to John Calvin, a wicked
city.

Calvin succeeded Zwingli; he was lean and hard,
young, and a social engineer, a tyrant and such a Puritan as dead Zwingli never thought of being.   Determined
to "purify" not only the Church and the State but
personal lives and habits as well, he laid upon Geneva a
hand of iron, and to the day he died never relaxed his
grip.   He turned Geneva into a city of spies, in which
brother spied on brother, and reported him; where every
item of private life was watched and flattered or condemned.   He made drastic, steel-jacketed laws on amuse-
ments, dancing, swearing, clothing, curfew, bookkeeping
and the combing of the hair.   He became a Protestant
pope: he piped, and the Genevans danced.   He domi-

nated the city, the nation, and in time, Europe. He became despotic, arbitrary, obstinate.

That is all most men know about John Calvin and all they care to know. Mention his name to a modern religious sophisticate, and there is a storm of abuse: "Calvin! An intolerant bigot! A moral busybody, making everybody's business his own. Puritan!" He may have been all of that; yet if that is all we see in Calvin, we see but half the man and we miss quite all of his real significance. The Dictator of Geneva was one of the great creative forces of history. "To omit Calvin from the forces of Western evolution," wrote Viscount Morley, "is to read history with one eye shut." This man, harsh and domineering as he was, was the organizer of the non-conformist conscience, the fountainhead of the Puritan strain.

Religiously, he gave us a new type of church. Luther had left a State Church behind him, even after he had struck off the galling shackles of Rome. His Germans were left to take their faith and their forms of worship from the princes under whom they happened to live. Government dominated Church, until Calvin came. He would not stand for the Lutheran idea. He broke clean with the secular power, refused to allow the Church to remain the tool of the State, stood for the right of every congregation to choose its own ministers and perform its own functions. He raised laymen to new positions of influence. Power begat power, a new self-respect for the laymen and a new disrespect for kings. When men began to understand, under the teaching of Calvinism, the doctrine of the "Sovereignty of God," they began to have less regard for the sovereignty of men. When they grasped the idea that they were the "chosen of God," they gathered courage to humble their kings, to worship as they pleased without fear of governmental interference. Wherever the Calvinists went, they stood like iron men for freedom, inspired to defend their rights against the tyranny of civil rulers, and to show that to be politically free men must first be religiously free.

Calvin thus built a new kind of State, made strong by non-conformist correction, shot through with the Puritan strain. The groundwork of effective democracy, of representative government, of popular sovereignty was laid in the "presbyterian" system by the Calvinists, who took into government the idea of the sovereignty of God and the independence of individual conscience. The government forms of the English-speaking people, not perfect, to be sure, but the most representative of any so far, are what they are largely because of the influence of Puritanism. Ex-President Coolidge, named "Calvin" by Puritan parents, said last year: "Our doctrine of equality and liberty, of humanity and charity, comes from our belief in the brotherhood of man through the fatherhood of God. The whole foundation of enlightened civilization, in government, in society and in business, rests on religion." He might well have said "rests on Geneva."

Intellectually, Calvin was a giant, and he left the footprints of a giant behind him. No system ever demanded so much of the thinking powers as Calvinism demands; no system has done as much to train and develop those thinking powers as Calvinism. Wherever you find Calvinism you find schools. Puritan academies in England, the parish schools of John Knox in Scotland, log-cabin schoolhouses on the New England shore are all by-products of the Puritan strain. A race of ministers not only heroic and devoted but also educated, passed through the portals of these schools, academies and colleges, with diplomas which were a passport anywhere in the educational world. They in turn inspired the lay mind to seek sure, rational, logical foundations for faith.

Morally, Calvin gave a new backbone to society. He labeled unchastity, so prevalent in his century, as plain repellent sin, robbing it of the doubtful honor of being "only human weakness," making it disgraceful and not excusable. Lying was abhorred, hyprocrisy and snobbishness were smothered in scorn. There came through the Calvinistic Puritan a stubborn sense of duty, an obstinate "righteousness" which burned like acid into the loose morality of the day. Calvinism was an uncompromising moral force which raised everywhere the standards of behavior, and strenuously tended to sobriety, generosity and stability.

Economically, we are indebted to John Calvin for the rise of the middle class and for capitalism. Work and thrift were watchwords in his code; idleness was disgraceful, the waster and the spendthrift were to be shunned. "No work, no eat," held for everybody. Work and thrift produced wealth. Wealth changed its name to "capital" and it became indispensable as the social and industrial order changed. Calvinists became capitalists. The Huguenot weavers, banished from France, influenced greatly the industrial development of England. All over Europe, and later in America, the Calvinist capitalist became identified with the trading, manufacturing, mercantile classes. There were certain evil results of this emphasis. A religious sanction was given to material gain, a divine right was given to private property, the blessings of the Church were given to the amassing of wealth. We are only beginning to see the evils of capitalism; yet it is a system necessary to our development.

Such is Calvinism and its fruits, good and bad. But with the evidence all in, one conclusion is self-evident. Calvinism produced a heroic race of men who have determined the course of human history. That race has conquered the wilderness, cleansed governments, purified social orders, fought revolutions, built manhood. John Calvin would be gratified could he come back to-day and hear a multitude of American Boy Scouts raise their hands in salute and solemnly swear: "I promise to keep myself physically strong, mentally awake and morally straight." That is just what Calvin would want them to say.

Geneva was a city of spies, a home for refugees and a base for missionaries. Disciples sat a while at the feet of the teacher, then scattered like a hail-storm over Europe. Down into the Netherlands they went, to fight with William of Orange against the Spanish Duke of Alva. That Dutch Revolt against Spanish and Catholic domination is without a parallel in history. Motley, in his *Rise of the Dutch Republic,* paid high tribute to Calvin: "It would be ridiculous to deny that the aggressive, uncompromising, self-sacrificing, intensely-believing, perfectly fearless spirit of Calvinism had been the animating soul, the motive power of that great revolt. For the Provinces to have encountered Spain and Rome without Calvinism, would have been to throw away the sword and fight with the scabbard."

Out of the Swiss mountains into fair France ran the Puritan strain. The French called them "Huguenots" and went after them with fire and sword. Open warfare broke out: the worst kind of warfare, marked by assassination, intrigue, banishment and massacre. It

was a gray day for France when her swords went red
with Huguenot blood. It was a fatal day when she
banished the Huguenots, for that mishap broke her
religious spine and her march of progress was delayed for
more than a century.

Over into Scotland flowed the stream. John Knox,
builder of parish schools and of the modern temper of
the Scot, rose to confront a Catholic Queen of Scots, to
drive her from the land, thus saving Scotland from
French rule and religious oppression. Knox was a mountain of strength; no man ever had a greater influence on
a nation than he has had on Scotland. He combined a
Calvinistic 'theology with Puritan practise, patriotic
with religious sentiment. He created a Scotch Presbyterian Church which has been a dominating influence in
the land of the heather, in America, and throughout the
English-speaking world as well.

The Calvinist next stormed England, where the road
had been cleared for him by the "Oxford Reformers,"
Erasmus, Colet and More. Erasmus, author of the famous Greek New Testament, was writing his *Dagger of
the Christian Soldier,* while Sir Thomas More was writing
Utopia. Both had running through them one golden
thread: that golden Reformation ideal that "the object
of all government is the common good of the whole people." They advocated what would seem modern to us,
taxation of the rich for the sake of the poor, universal

education, and the doctrine that the ideal government is a constitutional monarchy. John Colet was Dean of St. Paul's Cathedral, and a schoolmaster with advanced ideas. Sixteenth-century education needed him. He stopped the whipping and flogging of children in his schools, threw out the stale, inaccurate Latin of the monks and put in a fresh beautiful Latin and Greek imported from Italy; he actually made "grammar" attractive and easy to learn.

These three labored in the days of Henry VIII, that "bluff King Hal" who was every inch a king and never very much of a gentleman. Henry was at first a good Catholic, writing a treatise against Luther which earned for him the title "Defender of the Faith." Every king of England to this day has written that title after his name. But the time came when Henry wanted to divorce one wife and take another, and when the Pope said "No," then Henry ceased to be a Catholic. He broke off relations with Rome, divorced Catherine of Aragon and married Anne Boleyn. The discontent with papal usurpation reached a crisis when Henry was declared by Act of Parliament to be the head of the Church of England.

When Henry died, Edward VI, a nine-year-old boy, came to the throne. He was more Protestant than his father. Latin masses ceased, celibacy waned and priestly vestments were discarded as too "popish." Protestantism was winning, when suddenly the boy-king died, and

Mary, Catholic Mary, Bloody Mary, became queen. She had just cause to hate the Protestants, for her mother was the luckless Catherine of Aragon. Death to them leaped out from her frail white hand as she signed three hundred death-warrants in less than five years. Burnings, beheadings, torturings, blood, blood, blood. It took strong men to face Bloody Mary—but strong men were there. Puritanism, the heart and soul of which was Calvinism, met the iron of persecution with the iron of the Puritan strain. The Puritans stood fast during the Roman reaction, and they saved England.

Elizabeth followed Mary: Elizabeth, daughter of Henry and ill-fated Anne Boleyn. She brought Protestantism back into power though she detested the Puritan. She hated that group which would purify the English Church from within, and she hated more those who would break from it entirely to form other, nonconformist sects. Yet in spite of her opposition their numbers grew and their influence increased. Strange new names were passed from lip to lip: "Presbyterian," "Congregationalist," "Baptist," "Quaker." Puritans were driven out to Holland, and thence to America. Some managed to stay and fight the kings. Oliver Cromwell raised a motley army of "Ironsides," sent King Charles to the beheading block, and set up England's first and only Commonwealth.

England can never pay her debt to Cromwell. He

gave her the finest Court morally that she ever had. He fought back a rising tide of materialism, put the conscience of the sincere individual in the place of the blundering "divine" authority of the priests, and replaced the "divine" right of kings by a theory of Parliamentary supremacy. Democracy was cradled in Cromwell's camp, and political liberty had a good pioneer in him. After he died, the kings and the priests came back, but not with the power they had held before. They dug his corpse from the grave, hanged it and beheaded it and set up his head on a pole atop Westminster Hall. But they were too late. The harm had been done. The taint of Puritanism was in the blood of the Englishman, and there it has remained to this day.

A quarter of a century before the Commonwealth, a tiny boat called the *Mayflower* dropped anchor near what is now Cape Cod, on the Massachusetts coast. One hundred and two Calvinists crowded to the rails, and peered across the bay toward the bleak shore, where they were about to "bring forth on this continent a new nation, conceived in liberty and dedicated to the proposition that all men are created equal." The Eleven have followed the trail of old Columbus; their banners are to remain on shores which his left in defeat.

CHAPTER XV

NEW SHORES

THERE are two great roots to American civilization. These twin roots grew close together, and they were not only roots but impulses, motives, drives found in the breasts of all settlers and conquerors. One might be called the economic root; its growth and power are to be seen in the relentless push toward the West, in the search beyond the Atlantic for gold and fresh, green land. The other we might call religious, and is to be seen in the quest of the harried and the persecuted for God and freedom to worship God. Gold and God! They are the twin drives of American colonization. Those who came for the precious yellow dust found precious little of it, and that well mixed with the bitter dregs of disappointment and defeat. Those who came for God stayed to build an American nation, and to leave upon that nation the glory of their sacrificial scars and the vast influence of their spirit.

The Spaniard came first, wading ashore with a sword in his hand, a missionary priest at his back, dreams of fabulous wealth in his adventure-crazed brain. Ponce de Leon, Balboa, De Soto, Cortez, Coronado were all gold-seekers. California, Florida, the burning, empty plain of our great Southwest watched them come and go. New Spain could not be, could not win. No nation founded on greed and gluttony, with the missionary shoved always to the rear, can long endure. The roaring of the buccaneer conquered the pleading of the evangelist, and while fifteen millions in gold went back annually as treasure to Spain, the colonial hopes of the Don went with it. He gambled, and he lost.

Yet the missionary, hopelessly shouted down as he was, did much that was good. He stopped abruptly the bloody human sacrifices of the old Aztec religion of Mexico. He brought the Indian to worship in new and beautiful cathedrals, introducing him there to a new art and a new learning. He gave him schools for his children. One thousand Indian boys were enrolled in a single school in Mexico City; there was even a college for Indian girls. Grammars and dictionaries began to pour off the printing presses imported from Spain; booksellers and authors talked in groups in the streets. Surely, thousands of luckless Indians died beneath the cruel Spanish lash in the gold-mines of Potosi; but thousands more gained rights and privileges they had never had before the Spaniard came. The blood stream of the Mexican was colored for ever when the red Indian married the white daughter of the ruling class, and the future of the race was thereby profoundly affected.

All this happened, however, in Mexico and the South. To the north of Mexico, New Spain perished quickly. The only traces left of it to-day are a few ancient mission bells in California or Florida, tolling their matins and their vespers with a certain sad note of failure.

New France proved better and more enduring than New Spain. France sent not only adventurers to explore, but gay voyageurs to trap and build a trade in fur and Jesuits to plant the Cross of Christ. The Jesuits were the men of the Society of Jesus, a militant order founded by Ignatius Loyola, a contemporary of Martin Luther. They were the flying squadron, the shock troops of Rome and most effective in the counter-Reformation of the Roman Church. Organized and disciplined like the military, they went where they were told to go, never wondering why, asking only to do and die. They scattered out across India, Japan, the South Seas, North and South America. Father Marquette, Jesuit, rode in the lead canoe of Joliet, the gay explorer of the Mississippi, and his presence there is significant. The Jesuits led; they did not follow; they pushed out ahead of the explorers, intent on building blockhouses for France and finding souls for Christ. They went deep into the forest in search of the red Indian; they found the villages of the Mohawk, Huron and Iroquois. They faced, and they knew they faced, torture and ridicule and death at the hands of the savage. Yet they poured into the woods, determined to baptize a few of the red men into the Church ere death should come to them from the red man's hand. They had their fingers cut off with clam-shells, their eyes burned out with fire, their bodies torn and twisted and broken. Parkman tells of a Father Superior, in the midst of his suffering, writing home to France: "We shall die, we shall be captured, butchered: be it so. Those who die in their beds do not always die the best deaths. I see none of our company cast down." Whatever later Jesuitism may have been, here is stark heroism, missionary zeal that has never been surpassed.

What good did it do? A whole Indian nation, the "White Fish," threw away their fetishes, smashed their magic drums and appeared in the forest singing Christian hymns. Indian villages took Christian names, and the people in them began practising Christian morals. Jesuit Fathers went from one village to another, arbitrating differences and securing peace. They did not change the nature of the American Indian; they modified it. Parkman says again, "In the wars of the next century we do not find those examples of diabolic atrocity with which the earlier annals are crowded. The savage burned his enemies alive, it is true, but he rarely ate them; neither did he torment them with the same deliberation and persistency. He was a savage still, but not so often a devil. Thus King Philip's War in New England, cruel as it was, was less ferocious, judging from Canadian experience, than it would have been if a generation of civilized intercourse had not worn down the sharpest asperities of barbarism." Might not the whole scene of early American history been different if *all* early settlers had been as anxious for the soul of the Indian as they were for his land?

Yet the Jesuit failed, and New France failed. The fierce Iroquois wiped out the mission stations, and a greed for furs wiped out the hopes of a transplanted France. Political trickery and economic greed wrecked what might have been a splendid civilization, and the Frenchman soon withdrew from all but the tip of the continent. Then came the Englishman, intent not so much on gold or fur as he was on freedom to worship God and hold to his own faith. The Englishman stayed.

Cavaliers and Royalists, aristocrats and gentlemen came first. They had little or no quarrel with things in Old England, and they steered their ships for the South, toward the easy, even climate in the land of cotton, tobacco and far-flung plantations. They came to look for gold at first, but a few disastrous expeditions disrupted that dream and they settled down to building their homes and their churches in the soil of the new world. The green leaf of the tobacco plant soon turned to gold in their barns, and created a rich, cultured, aristocratic class of "Southerners" who have contributed

much to the life of the nation. Virginia became the
"Mother of Presidents," and gave to us as well the
"Father of his Country." Out of that South came
Patrick Henry of the silver tongue, with his immortal
"Give me liberty or give me death." From Monticello
came a fine gentleman who wrote the first sentence into
the Declaration of Independence: "We hold . . . that
all men are created free and equal," who held that
governments derive "their just powers from the consent
of the governed." Thomas Jefferson was the first
American Democrat, and his hand is seen in more than a
little of the structure of American democracy. Every
Presidential campaign since his day has heard something
of "Back to Jeffersonian democracy!"

Then came the *Mayflower*. Thirteen years after
Jamestown, the Pilgrim-Puritan arrived. The night
before he came ashore he drew up and signed a "Mayflower Compact" which was in reality the birth-
certificate of American democracy. It read: "In the
name of God, Amen; We, whose names are underwrit-
ten, having undertaken, for the glory of God, and ad-
vancement of the Christian faith, a Voyage to plant the
first colony in the northern parts of Virginia, do, in the
presence of God and one of another, covenant and com-
bine ourselves together into a Civil Body Politic, for
our better ordering and preservation, and furtherance
of the ends aforesaid, and, by virtue hereof, to enact,

constitute and frame such just and equal laws, ordinances, acts, constitutions, offices, from time to time, as shall be thought most meet and convenient for the general good of the Colony. . . ." "In the name of God" . . . "for the general good of the colony" . . . "having undertaken, for the glory of God" . . . "to plant the first colony." Here is no Magna Charta, with a king forced to sign; no compromise, no hard driven bargain between ruler and ruled. Here is a new concept of society, a new ideal of government, a new nation being born. Here is popular constitutional liberty, "humanity recovering its rights," as Bancroft put it. Here also is the final answer to men who say glibly that "Economic advantage and gain was the dominant motive of American colonization." That is true neither of the Pilgrims who drew up the Mayflower Compact nor of the thousands of Puritans who followed in the great Immigration of 1630-40, who later drew up their "New England Confederation" agreement with the opening sentence: ". . . we all came into these parts of America with one and the same end, namely, to advance the kingdom of the Lord Jesus Christ."

Their Puritan strain is in our blood for all time. In our society are Puritan ideals, in our morality a Puritan tinge, in our government the Puritan principle of equality and self-rule. Twenty-five million people in America to-day, one out of every five, one-fourth of the population of the United States, are descendants of the Puritan. But four-fourths of us, over one hundred and twenty millions, pay homage to him every day of our lives by the very manner in which we live. We shall never move out from under his shadow, nor escape his influence.

He gave us Thanksgiving Day. Once a year we stop work and worry in America and engage in a nation-wide day of prayer, because the ghost of the Puritan urges us. Once a year, in a nation where we have no established church or religion, we find the President and each state governor calling us back to the Christian ideals of the first builders. Catholic, Jew and Protestant are one on that day. Is there any other character in American history who has worked that miracle with us?

He gave us the public school, and his presence inhabits the schoolrooms of America, where our sons and daughters learn their "three R's." We should stop erecting more statues and plaques to the Puritan, and carve over the door of every schoolhouse in the land the legend, "Enter reverently, ye who seek knowledge. This school is a part of your Puritan heritage." The public school is his everlasting monument. May we write it indelibly on the mystic parchment of our hearts and minds that *the first public schools in all of human history were those of Puritan New England.* There was none in the Old England he had left; education there was the privilege of the few.   There was none even in the southern colonies of the new world, where education for years was left in the hands of tutors on the great plantations.   The New Englander, living a different life in his scattered towns, thought far differently.   He created the era of the free public school, and made education not the privilege of the fortunate but the duty of all, to be supported at the expense of the whole community.   Now turn back and read the educational ideals of Erasmus, Colet and More, and you will find the source of the Puritan ideal.

Nor did they stop with common schools.   Colleges grew in the wilderness.   Harvard was founded sixteen years after the first Pilgrim set foot on American soil, for the education of ministers.   After Harvard came William and Mary in Virginia, Yale in Connecticut, Princeton in New Jersey, King's College, now Columbia University, in New York.   *These were all church schools.* Until 1750, the College of Philadelphia, now the University of Pennsylvania, was the only school in the country founded independent of religious leadership.   By 1800 there were thirty colleges, and seventeen of them were church-founded and church-maintained.   If the American standard of education is the backbone of the American state, then the backbone of that standard is the Puritan spirit.

The Puritan flanked his schools and colleges with two

other weapons in his fight on ignorance: the printing press and the library. He imported trained printers from England, and soon had a flood of typically American literature flowing through the colonies. The first book printed in the new land was John Eliot's translation of the Bible into the Indian tongue. Private libraries were everywhere, and some of the finest in the world were in the possession of Puritan and southern gentlemen. It was only natural that these libraries should grow up, expand into community affairs. By 1763, according to James Truslow Adams, there were twenty-three public libraries from Maine to Georgia.

The Puritan shadow falls also across our system of political democracy. Deep in him was a faith in the capacity of men to govern themselves, native in him was a tendency toward self-government. That tendency found expression in the "town-meeting" of his colony, which furnished not only a good school in political action but in which were also the beginnings of our modern political caucus and convention. Here was no reliance on tradition and authority, but a genuine attempt at government of the people, by the people and for the people. Here was recognized no divine right but the divine right of character. We may say all we want of the intolerance of Puritan government; we can criticize him all we will for "burning witches" and "using the ducking stool"; but the facts show that the Puritan was

not so intolerant as his critics would have him. No
witch was ever burned in New England, and there is no
decent evidence that a ducking stool was ever used. This
"intolerance" is more slander than fact. It is quite true
that universal suffrage was not granted, and that
Church and State were united; it is also true that there
was more freedom and tolerance in New England than
there was, at the same moment, in the England the Puritan had just left. The settler of New England was no
true democrat; he distrusted democracy; yet in his
theories of government and in much after practise,
democracy was in process of evolution.

What the Puritan left undone, the men who broke
away from him tried to do, and in large measure, succeeded. Thomas Hooker rebelled against the methods
of government in Massachusetts and went out to found
the colony of Connecticut, and to become, to many men,
the "father of American Democracy." Hooker and his
men wrote a Constitution uniting the river towns of
Connecticut, which had tremendous influence on the
subsequent Constitution of the United States. Roger
Williams, the Baptist, expelled from Massachusetts,
brought into life the city of Providence, the state of
Rhode Island and the first complete religious freedom in
America. One can almost see him smiling at us out of
the epochal phrasing of the First Amendment: "Con-
gress shall make no law respecting the establishment of

religion, or prohibiting the free exercise thereof."

Others than Puritans, however, came to settle in America. Freedom lured them, oppression drove them, and Christian fortitude supported them. It would almost seem that He who had walked the shores of Galilee now walked the shores of America, calling across to the broken and disheartened in Europe, "Come unto me, all ye who are weary and heavy-laden." They came, in multitudes. William Penn, Quaker son of a fighting British admiral, led his Quakers into New Jersey and Pennsylvania, to found colonies which were really great religious and philanthropic enterprises. Penn made a treaty with the Indians, which stands to-day as one of the noblest mile-stones in American history; a treaty which is said to be "the only one never sworn to, and the only one ever kept." He treated the Indian as a Christian brother, and he won him completely! The Dutch came, bought the island of Manhattan for twenty-four dollars, established their Reformed Church on American soil and gave way quickly to the Englishman, passing on to us a belief in Santa Claus, colored Easter eggs, voting by ballot and *representative* democracy. Lutherans from Sweden settled along the Delaware, and Scotch-Irish filtered into the middle colonies. A few Huguenots settled in the South, and the Catholics under Calvert and Baltimore set up in Maryland a state so anxious for religious tolerance that they allowed no

man to call another by a religious nickname! Oglethorpe, a soldier, a gentleman and surely a Christian,
founded Georgia, a colony remarkable for its immediate
prohibition of rum and slavery, for its taverns which
closed on Sunday that the colonists might be in church,
for its pious Moravians, as sternly spiritual as the Puritan of the North, for its kilted Scottish Highlanders, and
for its helping hand extended to the unfortunate debtors
of old London.

Puritanism narrowed, waned and weakened. It lost
vitality and control in England when Oliver Cromwell's
son threw up his hands and quit. It lost out gradually
in America, where it became bitter, pedantic and stale.
It stood in need of a revival of the zeal and passion of
the Eleven for the souls of men, in need of the revival
of the spirit of the Galilean volunteers whose vision was
directed outward, upon others, rather than inward, upon
themselves. Revival came, on both sides of the Atlantic,
from a friend of Oglethorpe who just then was riding
horseback through England, jostling the fate of nations
in his saddle-bags.

CHAPTER XVI

THE MAN ON HORSEBACK

IN 1734 George Washington celebrated his second birthday and General James Oglethorpe, Governor of Georgia, went home to England for rest and recruits. Of rest he got almost none at all, but of recruits he got a great abundance. Felons and ex-felons, debtors in the jails and outcasts on the street sought him out and begged him to give them their second chance in his colony beyond the sea. They won his heart while he in turn was winning the heart of London. He walked the streets of that old city in company with Chief Tomo-chi-chi and a half-dozen American Indians. Six feet tall they were bronzed and proud, unafraid of the roar of London's traffic, unawed by the majesty of England's King when they were presented at his Court. London went mad over the savages, stood in crowds on tiptoe to look at them. Somewhere in those surging crowds we might have found two young preacher-brothers just out of Oxford. Charles Wesley might have been there, with his brother John.

The Wesleys met Oglethorpe, and talked with him about Georgia and the Indians. The red man was a splendid man, said Oglethorpe, with a noble soul that he considered well worth saving. Georgia and the Georgians were splendid, too, but some of them were rough and hard to handle. Good churches would help a lot in the colony; the preaching of Christ would help. Would the Wesleys like to go to Georgia? They would. They sailed. They failed. Charles, who went as the Governor's secretary, fell ill. John, who went to preach to the whites and to save the soul of the Indian, fared even worse. The whites did not take kindly to his preaching and his mannerisms; the Indians listened stolidly, and were not convinced. Poor John Wesley became bitter toward them, calling them flatly, "gluttons, thieves, dissemblers, liars, murderers." The brothers soon returned to England, sadder but wiser men, failures, both of them. They should have been crushed. But they were too British for that. They settled down instead to become two of the most valuable men of the eighteenth century. Charles led a renaissance of inspired popular music, became the troubadour of modern sacred song, gave wings to a singing revival of religion. John preached, and preaching saved England from the horrors of the French Revolution by saving the Englishman from his sins. John Wesley directed a bloodless revolution that has been of greater blessing than all the victories won by gun and sword.

Sin had a good start on the Wesleys; it had been in

the saddle for a long time. The Industrial Revolution was coming to the United Kingdom, upsetting the whole social, economic and moral life of the people, drawing them away from the farms to live like huddled sheep in close quarters in the city. Crowding brought poverty, unemployment, deprivation, debasement, demoralization. Every sixth house in crowded London was a "pub," a grog-shop, a saloon. Gin drinking was the curse of all ranks of society, eating like fire the vitality of the race. Signs over the "pubs" read, "Drunk for a penny, dead drunk for tuppence," and the men and women of the masses, seeking to drown their sufferings in gin and rum, spent their pennies fast. Fathers and mothers, who labored from daylight to dark for a wage of sixty to ninety cents *a week,* were drunk from Saturday night to Monday morning, abandoning their children to the streets, the gutter and the jail. Bull-baiting, cock-fighting, prize-fights between women were the sport of degenerate mobs. Bands of ruffians became expert at rioting and arson, and one gang gathered regularly every Sunday afternoon to roll women down-hill in hogsheads. Dick Turpin, that premier of highwaymen, staged his daring holdups in the broad light of day; coaches were robbed in Piccadilly and Leicester Square. England was alive with crime and criminals. She had a list of one hundred and sixty crimes punishable by hanging. The crowd liked hangings; they came by the

thousand to watch the public executions of mere boys
who had done no more than pick a pocket or steal a sheep
or cut down a tree in an orchard. Jails and prisons
were loathsome filthy holes in which the luckless prisoners rotted slowly, and compared with which the gallows
seemed an easy punishment.

What had happened to the English? How could
England come to such a day? Some say it was due to
the Industrial Revolution; others that it was "just one
of those periods of decline." Good reasons, but not con-
clusive. The real reason is that religion had become a
subject of ridicule in England. *And wherever you find
irreligion and a church with lost influence, you find
social decay and moral insensibility.* When the fox-
hunting parsons of Old England deserted their flocks to
follow their hounds, or to engage in drinking bouts,
their flocks simply followed their lead. When they repeatedly preached from the text, "Be not righteous
overmuch," then righteousness went out of the people's
hearts as water goes over a dam. Religion had lost its
warmth, its heat, its power. Waning Puritanism had
lost its grip; the Established Church had a heart gone
cold as stone. The higher classes laughed at religion,
the lower ignored it. Christianity seemed a lost cause,
Christ a lost hope, and the Eleven Men were fighting
with their backs to the wall. Is it any wonder that the
Wesleys were booed, pelted with stones and mud and

rotten eggs, when their preaching stirred the fires of faith again?

John Wesley literally leaped into the saddle. He bought a horse, stuffed his saddle-bags with books, and rode grimly out to joust with England's evil. He rode forty-five hundred miles a year, two hundred and fifty thousand miles in all before he finally stepped down out of the saddle. He was up at four in the morning, he had preached by five, by seven he was off down the road to his second preaching-point, reading and studying as he rode. He preached from two to five sermons a day for over fifty years, better than forty-two thousand in all. He rode in the rain and winter winds, he swam his horse across swollen angry rivers, he traveled roads infested with highwaymen and murderers, he took his life in his hands a hundred times as he faced belligerent, excited mobs. And this man never weighed more than one hundred and twenty pounds in his life! He rode and he preached in the wreck-strewn wake of the Industrial Revolution and made his way into the heart of England. He has been called "a vitalized shuttlecock, weaving the destiny of England."

Only a few came to hear him at first. Then hundreds. Then thousands and tens of thousands. His audiences spread out over the fields and hillsides like great hungry flocks of sheep. He preached, at seventy years of age, to twenty and thirty thousand people a day. Dirty-faced

miners from the Cornwall mines; half-dead laborers
from the factory and the mill; owners of mills and
managers of factories, responsible for such conditions
and mildly curious about his preaching, rubbed shoulders
with their victims, the human wrecks who were perish-
ing for the lack of it. To all of them he preached, "Re-
pent ye, for . . ." and, "*Now* is the day of salvation."
He drove into the hearts of the despondent masses the
exhilarating thought that in them, oppressed and
broken as they were, were divine possibilities; they were
the children of God, loved by Him though oppressed
by men; they were sinners, to be sure, but sinners who
might be saved by a single act of faith in Christ. He
drew thousands of those beaten ones to their knees in
a new devotion to righteousness; he swept other thousands of the higher classes to their knees side by side with
the lowly.

Lord Palmerston, it is said, arose one morning during
an evangelical sermon in his church, and stalked furiously out of the place, muttering to himself that things
had "come to a fine pass when religion could intrude
into a man's private life." Wesley struck hard at the
Palmerston type of mind; he knew that religion *had* to
be personal before it could be anything else. He knew
that personal faith had its social results, and he knew
also that keen minds like Palmerston's were to blame for
much of the social degradation of England. He thus

proceeded to fire the finest minds of England with the
thought that religion and religionists were responsible for
all righteous and unrighteous living. He actually made
the best men of England wonder if *they* were not responsible, themselves, for the condition of the worst men
of England. He made them search their hearts and ask
themselves the old question of the Eleven, "Lord, is it
I?" He blazed out at slave-holders who were also pew-
holders, and made them see the ethical consequences of
their "religion"; he gave a spiritual dynamic to the fight
against the trade in African slaves. He struck as hard
at the intemperance of the "classes" as he did at the gin
drinking of the masses. He shamed a lot of gin-drinking
ministers back into their pulpits and he shamed a lot of
soberness into the nation at large. He began to fight
the liquor traffic with organizations instead of with
scattered individuals. He championed everywhere the
rights of labor against the cruelties of industrialism,
loaning capital for small enterprises, founding free labor
bureaus, giving to the modern labor movement a spiritual quality. A legion of men and women, stirred by
his preaching, left their quiet comfortable pews and went
to preach the hope of Christ in the jails. Prison reform
took on new life while Wesley ranged the land. He
built refuges for widows and he organized Strangers'
Societies; he founded medical dispensaries and orphanages, and he became the real father of popular and in-

expensive libraries for the poor. He awoke England socially by first awakening her spiritually.

Down in Gloucester a rich fellow with a swagger and a velvet coat and a heart of gold caught a gleam of what Wesley meant and sent it down into Sooty Alley, where the chimney-sweeps lived. Robert Raikes was interested in the waifs of the Alley, and he feared for them. He watched them play in the streets while they were abandoned by their drunken parents; he saw them thrown into jail for crimes that were not their fault; he studied them and he saw that unless things changed, Gloucester and England would have on their hands a generation of illiterate little savages. So he proceeded to *do* something: he gathered together a score of the toughest urchins in England, and led them down a muddy street in Gloucester straight into the first Sunday-school. He had hired a Mrs. Critchley, ex-manager of a pub, and therefore adept at corporal punishment, to teach them Bible verses and the catechism and, may we never forget it, how to read and spell and write. We honor Raikes to-day as the father of the Sunday-school. As a matter of fact he sought to lay the foundations of elementary secular knowledge as well as to teach the doctrines of religion. He did his work well; others copied him and his Gloucester school. The Queen sent for him to come to Windsor and tell her more about his work. Catherine of Russia asked him to establish

Sunday-schools in her cold land; the French wanted him
to come to France; everybody wanted him; everybody
got him. To-day his schools belong to all of us; they are
found from pole to pole. Thirty million children enrolled in them might rise and call him blessed. And a
legion that never can be counted, who have passed
through the portals of the Sunday-school, acknowledge
that he founded the finest character-building institution
that civilization has ever known.

Good son of Wesley, too, in a later century, was
William Booth, that soldier of the Cross who left the
Church to preach from a soap-box on London's East
Side. An army fell in step behind him, a "Salvation
Army" of rebuilt wrecks snatched from the very doors
of hell. They marched behind "General" Booth to the
tune of deep bass drums and blaring bands of brass, down
into the deepest lairs of sin; they pitched their gospel
tents in the heart of the reeking slums. Like Wesley
they sought out the half-beaten and the sick of soul. Did
not the Great Physician come to minister unto the sick?
They rallied them under the old banner of the Cross with
a new battle-cry: "A man may be down, but he's never
out." The pounding of those drums, the marching of
those singing battalions of the Lord, have been heard
around the world; wherever you find sin in a crowded
city you will find a "Lassie" fighting it. The Salvation
Army has proved to be a social weapon of mighty

lifting power, mighty socially because it is so sound spiritually.

We think of Wesley as English. We are wrong. He is no more strictly British than Jesus is strictly Jewish. He has crashed through the fences of mere nationalism, and he belongs more to the ages than to his age. From his seat on his wandering horse he cried, "The *world* is my parish." He meant it. He sent his followers across the seas in a new burst of missionary enthusiasm. In 1773 he wrote to George Shadford, a convert, "I let you loose, George, on the great continent of America." Little did he know that he was letting loose in America a religious hurricane, just in the nick of time. For America was expanding, growing by leaps and bounds. Especially did it expand after the Revolution was fought and won. Out across the Alleghanies, toward Ohio and Indiana, upon the great prairies of the West, America began to move. Westward went the pioneers and the wagon-trains, whither the course of American empire took its way; and westward, thank God, toward the new frontier, rode the saddle-bags men, the circuit-rider sons of England's Man-on-Horseback.

Over the entrance to the New York City General Post Office is the motto, "Neither snow nor rain nor heat nor gloom of night stays these couriers from the swift completion of their appointed rounds." That motto is a worthy tribute to the carriers of America's mail. It might well have been carved over the doors of the frontier church in tribute to the circuit riders. They rode thousands of miles alone, chased by fierce wolves in the forests, mobbed by human wolves in the crude, rough-and-ready towns. They rode into many a "Hell's Half Acre" and into many a "Devil's Gulch," and left them law-abiding, peaceful communities; they created the will to peace where gun-play had been king. They exercised exactly the same gentle, modifying, integrating influence on the new "barbarians" of America's "no-man's land," that the church of the Dark Ages had once had upon the barbarians of old Europe. Look where you will in the record of America's expansion, turn to whatever page in the history of her growth, from the tiny thirteen colonies to the world power she is to-day, and you will find the finger-prints, the handiwork, the ennobling influence of the minister of Jesus Christ.

Back in the Eastern States, too, things were happening. When Puritanism waned and died, according to some as early as 1660, a fresh flood of spiritual leaven was waiting to burst upon them. Jonathan Edwards, thundering preacher of Northampton, became a Prometheus carrying the sparks of the English awakening to New England; he kindled fires so fierce that half the nation trembled. George Whitefield, comrade of Wesley, with "a voice that could be heard a mile when he preached," met the coarse, raw tendencies of life in a wild America with a preaching that burned like vitriol. Revivalists among the Presbyterians built Princeton in New Jersey, and a Roman Catholic priest joined hands with a Protestant preacher to found the University of Michigan.

Such is the record of one-hundred-and-twenty-pound John Wesley, who failed so miserably in Georgia. He died in 1791, having kept the faith and having run a good race. He left behind him a "Methodist" church now numbering better than twelve million souls, which was something of a reenforcement for the battle-scarred Eleven who still led the march. More important even than this visible church is a fertile idea which he left germinating in the hearts of men of all creeds and sects: that the social order in which they lived was as good or as bad as their religion was good or bad. He actually made men believe that the condition of the worst of us was the fault of the best of us.

CHAPTER XVII

FRONTAL ATTACK

THE Wesleyan Awakening taught men to look in two directions: in, upon themselves; and out, upon others. It led them to search and make clean their own hearts, and to test their faith by the fruits of their own lives. It made them look out upon mankind and mankind's world, to consider that world as their parish, and it sent them down to the uttermost parts of the sea in search of "the worst of us." The subsequent movements of Christianity likewise went out in two directions: Men at home, in the West, set about the building of a sincerely Christian order of society in their own lands, while others ventured out to the outposts of civilization, north, south, east and west, to preach Christ where He had never been preached before.

That wave of missionary enthusiasm caught up William Carey from a cobbler's bench in England, led him to close for ever the door of his little shop that he might throw open the door to India. It snatched up David Livingstone out of a Scotch mill, where he was tending a spinning jenny, and sent him hurrying to open the door through which Christ and the white race poured into deepest, darkest Africa. These two were the first to ride the wave, and after them came a flood of lesser (?) stars to light the missionary horizon, to throw their light well into the darkness of superstition, ignorance and fear, to burn themselves out for Christ, and who now "lie buried in the corner of some forgotten field that is for ever"—God's. To write of all of them would be to write an encyclopedia of heroism, and even that, once written, would be a poor enough memorial. They and their fellow-laborers have been soldiers braver than Napoleon and Washington, winning victories of greater moment than Waterloo and Concord Bridge. They have conquered continents, races, worlds. They have been rebuilding the earth, reshaping international society.

They are not only preachers, these missionaries; some of them are medical men, turning back disease and the death-rate at the point of the lancet. Once the natives of India "fought" cholera by beating tin pans in the streets at midnight; now the Christian doctor has all but conquered it with vaccine and sanitation. He is stopping it, say some observers, as a ranger stops a prairie fire: *almost on a given line.* Hospitals have been built from pole to pole, and the first real vision of the great white Christ that has come to many a "heathen" has been the vision of the white-jacketed missionary doctor. The witch doctor and the man of magic are passing; the merciful hand of God is more surely seen in the hand of the operating surgeon than it ever was in the filthy paw of the begging holy man.

Some of them are scientific farmers, turning back famine at the point of the plow. Once famine was taken for granted in the East; now irrigation ditches form a network on the land, and bumper crops forestall starvation. Once the cattle of the Orient died in herds during the lean days when there was no food; now that same cattle-breeder has learned the use of the silo, and he stores his fodder against the evil day.

And some of them are teachers, dispensing knowledge. Education, anywhere, is a great leveler and a great up-lifter. Education is also dynamite. It has been passed around liberally, in the mission schools, and it has wrought havoc. It has broken the paralyzing grip of tradition in non-Christian lands. It has shaken the system of caste and sooner or later will wipe it out completely. It has filled the East with a new kind of man, who in coming to grips with Western learning has found the secrets of Western social progress and of Eastern social decay, and who is gradually taking over the reins of power and control wherever he may live. At his side stands a new woman, an emancipated woman, who like the man has caught a glimpse of the new horizons. Turkish and Mohammedan women are breaking out of the time-honored harem, and they are tearing off their veils. Chinese women have long since formed a "Heavenly Foot Society," at the instance of a missionary, and ceased to bind their feet. They are registered now at Wellesley and Vassar. Once the Chinese man asked of a prospective bride, "How long are her feet?" Now he asks, "Where did she go to school?" That realization of ability and equality never came out of the dead religions of the East: it came out of Christianity. The dynamite has exploded; the pot is boiling. Restlessness and revolution are everywhere. The East no longer sits in docile meditation as the legions from the West thunder over her; she is crowding her way swiftly into the council chambers of the world's Great Powers. One can not teach Christ and brotherhood in Christ without revolutionary results.

Momentous as these stirrings in the East have been, it is back to the West that we must turn in these late years, to touch the pulse of greatest Christian influence. Here we find that the years of the closing eighteenth and of the opening nineteenth centuries were years in which mankind, with its social, religious and economic institutions, reached a sharp turn in the road. The Frenchman whirled around the turn, in the mad rush of a red Revolution, upsetting his institutions completely, screaming with laughter as his king slipped off into oblivion and death. The Englishman took the corner a bit more carefully, picking his way gingerly along with the new machines of his Industrial Revolution, and guarding his time-honored institutions with that jealous care which is peculiar to him. The Americans staggered around the curve, weak from loss of blood at Bunker Hill and York-town, but with *his* institutions quite safe; they were as yet too strong and young to be seriously harmed. To all of them, things looked different once the hard turn had been made.

Government was different; politically, men had been reborn. Europe saw commoners fight their way up from the lowest ranks of society to sit on the old thrones of kings. The United States put a Virginia surveyor in the President's chair. The suffrage was extended. Un-touchables voted and made speeches in revamped parlia-ments. Education was extended, became a public duty and a universal privilege. Industry did an about-face. New factories belched forth smoke which shut off the sky and the horizons of a multitude of plodding laborers. Only yesterday they were proud artizans, but now their days were spent producing wealth for those who were already wealthy, while they themselves starved and shook their bright new chains in despair. It was a world turned upside down, revealing a totally new set of problems that men had never met before. It was a sur-prise attack on religion and morals. Good it is for us that the Eleven Men and their followers were not caught sleeping in their tents. They studied the field where the new battle was to be fought, planned a new strategy, changed their front and moved out to the attack.

That shift, or change of front, was a vital step. It had to come. Hitherto the primary objective of Christianity had been the individual. He and his soul were the beginning and the end of it all. But now men began to see that this saving of the individual soul was good, but not good enough. They began to realize, as one put it, that "if religion ends with the individual, it ends." They saw that to convert a man and send him out to live as a Christian in a social and economic order which was definitely anti-Christian, was like sending a man out to walk alone in a forest filled with beasts. It was absurd to salvage a soul from wreck while the evil which caused the wreck was allowed to go on unchecked. It will never do, for instance, simply to save a drunkard here and there, and then sit back complacently while the flood of alcohol pours on, making drunkards faster than we can find them. That would be like building a dam along the shores of a river where it does no good, instead of in the center of the stream. What was needed was a frontal attack on the *sources* of social evil. Evil must be struck down while it is still young and undeveloped, not when it has gained the strength of maturity.

So Christianity undertook a new maneuver, and proceeded to lay the ax to the root of the tree by *educating* and *legislating* definitely against the sources of the trouble. Its forces moved directly on the parliaments to build from the bottom up a new social order which should be really Christian. We may or may not approve of that mode of attack, may or may not think well of religion's assault on government and politics. But it would be good for some of the bitter critics to remember that for hundreds of years business and industry have pursued exactly the same course, influencing their way to profits. Corrupt politicans have whispered with lobbying thieves to loot the public purse, and any one with an "ax to grind" or a dollar to make has been perfectly free in influencing legislation. And while all this has been going on, the only disinterested group, with no ax to grind except the uplift of the race and with no stake to make save a better world to live in, has been the Christian Church. Standing squarely out against the sordid record of men who influenced law for gold is the clean record of the Christian, who has sought to influence it in order that life might be more abundant.

Before John Wesley was dead, men were at it. John Howard was peering into the dungeons of England's prisons, talking with jailers and executioners and with the shackled, scurvy-ridden wretches whom the law had imprisoned and forgotten. John Howard was standing in England's Parliament, telling the incredulous lawmakers of what he had seen in their bastiles, until he made them ashamed of themselves. His hour of triumph came when legislation was enacted to curb the stealing of jailers, to provide efficient medical care for the sick prisoners, to attack the "Hulks," those floating hells which transported felons to Botany Bay on the other side of the world. No man has done more to wipe out the complacent brutality of society toward the criminal than John Howard, Puritan contemporary of John Wesley. Wherever you see a modern prison you see the influence of this quiet little man who fought the lawlessness of the law with the weapon of better laws. Wherever you see prison hospitals, prison schools, clean and sunlit cells, you see the handiwork of this Christian reformer who would not consider the criminal as a beast to be whipped, but as a man to be redeemed. Frail and sickly, he might have spent his life in an easy search for health; rich, he might have wasted his substance. But God drove him and a sacred mission claimed him until his death. He hurried through England, France, Flanders and Holland on what Pitt called "a voyage of discovery, a circumnavigation of charity." He rushed in where angels, lawyers, doctors, and pseudo-reformers feared to tread. And he shook fearfully the house of human crime.

When John Howard died and society became careless again, Elizabeth Fry stepped into the breach. Elizabeth was a Quaker. She said "thee" and "thou." She

dared to say to the king of France: "When thee builds
a prison, thee had better build it with the thought ever
in thy mind that thee and thy children may occupy the
cells." Bold language, from a woman to a king. But
Elizabeth Fry was a bold woman. She went courageously
into old Newgate Prison, where the preachers of the
day read prayers to the prisoners, at a safe distance from
the bars. The fierce woman convicts of Newgate
reached through those bars one day, caught hold of a
minister, and tore every shred of clothing from his back.
But the little Quaker went boldly into their midst, read
Scripture and prayed with them, soon had them down
on their knees and praying for themselves. She gathered
their children into a whitewashed room and held school
for them, while their mothers huddled in silent groups
outside the door. She forced the government to make
the cells of Newgate clean, to give the women mat-
tresses to sleep upon, decent food to eat, female jailers
instead of men. Then she toured Europe in the foot-
steps of John Howard, and found herself received
cordially by kings and State ministers who wanted advice. They listened to her, knowing that she had within
her the Quaker Inner Voice which is the voice of God.
God bless her. God bless them. The crowns of the
Quakers must be bright in heaven. For three centuries
we have laughed at them and sneered at them, gone after
them with fire and sword, hanged them and cut off

their ears and whipped them at our cart-tails. Yet of all our Protestant sects they have been most energetic and faithful in the matter of social reform; they have stood like rock against war and child labor and intemperance and slavery. They have been, truly, the salt of the earth.

This nineteenth century produced another Christian miracle: the abolition of slavery from the British Empire. John Wesley, six days from death, put in the post a letter to a certain "William Wilberforce, M. P.," in which he said, among other things, "Go on, in the name of God." It was a gallant throwing of the torch from the hands of an old warrior to a new. William Wilberforce was just then fighting in Parliament to rid England of this curse which he and Wesley mutually hated, the curse of the trade in African slaves. Its horrors were a smothering weight on the heart of the young M.P. He found himself in agony at the thought of those slave ships coming up to the British Colonies with their cargoes of stolen and kidnaped blacks, chained and packed like animals in their holds. The thought of it took him out of the fashionable social whirl of the wealthy class of London and into a bitter fight against the traffic in human flesh. His gay companions laughed at him when he left them for the Negro; he was cold-shouldered, ridiculed and insulted; he heard lies spread abroad about his personal morals; his life was threatened by the irate

traders who had found money thicker than blood.
But he was Christian, an "Evangelical," to be exact.
He fought the cruelest fight that any man has ever
been called upon to enter, and he won. In 1807 a law
was passed by Parliament, in which the slave trade was
"utterly abolished, prohibited, and declared to be un-
lawful." In 1833, as he lay on his death-bed, news came
to him that another law had set free the last slave in the
Empire, and that Lord Stanley had said in the House of
Lords, as the bill was passed, "When Mr. Wilberforce
hears of it, he may well exclaim, 'Lord, now lettest Thou
Thy servant depart in peace!'" So passed slavery out
of the ken of the Englishman; or rather, so was slavery
driven out of his ken by William Wilberforce, Evangelical Anglican, who thought of his task as religious and
of himself as religiously called to perform it. He has
done more than any other modern for international
amity and for friendship and equality between the races.

Wilberforce freed the black, but he died and left the
whites still enchained. Women and girls were chained
to cars of coal in the mines, dragging them, on hands
and knees, through the long dark tunnels. Under-
nourished, pale-faced youngsters slaved at the looms of
the cloth-makers and the weavers, growing old before
their time. Terrified boys were impressed as chimney-
sweeps, forced up hot, stifling, gas-filled chimneys by
master-sweeps, who cared little whether they came

down again dead or alive. This industrial slavery brought worry to another rich young ruler, one Anthony Ashley Cooper, the Seventh Earl of Shaftesbury. In his journal he wrote frequently, "Anxious, very anxious, about my sweeps." The Earl became president of a "Climbing-boys Society," collected a vast and terrible evidence of death and ill treatment, of the buying and selling of children, and thrust it under the noses of every parliamentarian in London. They were indifferent; Shaftesbury was persistent. He enlarged on his work for the climbing-boys, and went about examining labor conditions in the mills, exploring factories, sitting down to talk in lodging houses and thieves' haunts and workers' homes, listening to their side of the story, studying their conditions and the causes of this misery, suffering with them and for them. Out of that benevolent slumming came such a mountain of evidence as even the parliamentarians dared not disregard. His efforts were rewarded in the passage of laws which brought the women and children out of the mines, reduced the inhuman hours of labor in the factories, put a curb on the exploitation of the poor by the rich, and drove the figure of the sooty-faced climbing-boy out of the English scene for ever. The Earl of Shaftesbury, factory reformer, Evangelical and lover of humanity, was a great humanitarian surgeon, divinely called to transform the face of industrial England, and he did it by way of the law.

These three were pioneers of the new day, first
leaders of the new attack. When they were gone a
host rose to carry forward their work. Charles Dickens
was so stirred by the cry of the children that he made the
world weep over *Oliver Twist* and *Nicholas Nickleby*.
Florence Nightingale, stirred by the cry of the sick, and
the moaning of men wounded in war, went off to the
Crimean War to lay the foundations of modern nursing.
Hospital nurses since then have walked in the shadow of
the Cross, and they ever will. The sisterhood of pity to
which they belong was founded by this "lady-with-the-
lamp-in-her-hand," who did it because "God called her
to His service." Then there were the men who heard the
cry of the working class for justice. The preachers,
Maurice, Kingsley and Scott Holland, joined hands with
Thomas Hughes, John Ludlow and other laymen and as
Christian Socialists they pleaded unceasingly for a living
wage for the worker in the name of a Carpenter from
Galilee. James Keir Hardie, who died in 1915 of heart-
break over the coming of the Great War, entered the
House of Commons in a tweed jacket and cloth cap to
represent the Labor Party from Scotland, and declared
that if he could live his life over again he would devote
it to the advocacy of the gospel of Christ. There was
Robert Hall, Baptist preacher, and defender of trade
unions at a time when to defend them meant ostracism;
Thomas Chalmers, Presbyterian, who established and

extended charity on a scientific basis; Edward Denison, Canon Barnett and others from Oxford, who founded Toynbee Hall in destitute Whitechapel and ushered in the era of the social settlement.

In Philadelphia Dr. Benjamin Rush started the fight against the saloon and intemperance. After his death Frances Willard seized the banner and carried it at the head of her Women's Christian Temperance Union, to be joined twenty years later by the Anti-Saloon League. These two groups represented "the Church in action against the saloon" and together, with American industry as aide, they have finally outlawed the liquor traffic from America. We who are still in the midst of the fight over the enforcement of prohibition may or may not agree with the methods of the leaders who won that fight for us; but even to a disinterested observer it must occur that the Christian forces struck at alcohol in the right place, at the source of supply. When they drove the shaft of an impregnable law deep into the heart of the brewing industry, they were cutting at the roots of the vilest social curse that the nation has ever known.

We were not so fortunate as England in getting rid of slavery. In the United States it took a civil war, tragic, dramatic and entirely unnecessary. Had the religious impulses in the American breast been as strong as the economic, and had the Church presented a united front, the Civil War would never have divided us. How

strong the influence of the Church was in those days
may be sensed in the exclamation of Henry Clay when
he heard that the Methodist Episcopal Church had split
over slavery.   Clay's face went white as he exclaimed,
"My God, that means war!"   The Church might have
prevented it, but the Church did not.   Not only the
Methodist, but the Baptists and Presbyterians as well,
were disrupted by the slavery dispute!   War came, long
years after Clay was dead and moldering in his grave,
and after fanatic John Brown's body was moldering in
his.   Yet time—and Christ—have healed most of the
old scars.   On the very site of John Brown's fort at
Harper's Ferry is a school for Negro youth.   A good
indication, perhaps, that the Christ who was crucified
afresh in that bloody conflict is slowly but surely overcoming the world.

After that war we enter the strictly modern era, and
we begin to hear of more of the aggressive social prophets.   These men are the disciples of Washington
Gladden of Columbus, and of that grand old prophet of
Rochester, Walter Rauschenbusch.   They are preachers
dissatisfied with a limited program of "two-sermons-
and-a-prayer-meeting-a-week," and who find themselves driven out to aid wherever life, liberty and the
pursuit of happiness are denied.   To them, the old
doctrine of resignation to the status quo as "the will of
God" is obsolete and gone.   Obedience to that will is not

by passive submission, but by a hard battle against everything that impedes the march of the Kingdom of God.
Ministers to-day are going to jail in defense of the rights
of labor; they are fighting for industrial democracy and
justice; they are demanding a more equal distribution
of wealth in a world held in strangle-hold by capitalism;
they have become prophets fighting the profit-motive
and the acquisitive instinct, building dams of spiritual
reality against a rising wave of materialism. Above
all and most important of all, they are fighting a grim
war against war. When Kirby Page sent out a question-
naire, last year, to the ministers of America to determine
their attitude on war and peace, he found that there
were no less than ten thousand preachers in this country
who had turned their backs for ever on the abominable,
inexcusable, organized murder which we call war; they
will never again support a war between peoples or nations, in any form whatsoever. They are vilified,
slandered and threatened, but even the most determined
of the militarists are afraid of their influence. They
may be "yellow pacifists" to some whose patriotism is
stereotyped or professional, but we had better help them
win their fight. They are facing up to the greatest
problem of our generation. Unless they win, the
Churches will close their doors and we shall all go down
in a new world catastrophe. They may find some satis-
faction in the thought that they have helped. One

hundred and forty-three thousand local churches and twenty millions of people have presented a united front in the Federal Council of the Churches of Christ in America not only to fight war, but to strike down oppression, ignorance, injustice and slavery wherever they rear their ugly heads.

"The defense rests!" So say our lawyers in the courts when their evidence is in and their pleading done. Christianity rests her case on this evidence, from Pentecost to the present hour. Sketchy and incomplete as it is here presented, it yet seems to show that civilization, without the salt and light of Christian influence, could never have reached the peak on which it rests to-day. Jesus Christ, with the Church and the Christian as His tools, has tempered and cast that civilization in the blazing forges of time. He has given to it its power and glory, its purest virtue and noblest institutions. He has saved it, time and time again, from total collapse, and to-day He is fighting the deep-seated causes of collapse. He has fought slavery in its many forms, helped us toward democracy and whatever genuine equality and brotherhood we have ever had. His Spirit has fought an unceasing battle for the innocent weak against arrant wrong, given a spiritual drive to the upward movements of labor and the working class, and developed a splendid sense of chivalry out of the base stuff of feudalism.

The Spirit of Christ has elevated womanhood, en-

nobled marriage, abolished infanticide, protected childhood, blessed the family. It has produced an enviable
art, sculpture, literature and music. It has fostered and
preserved learning, squared itself with every advance
of wisdom and intelligence, evolved for us the university
and the public school. It has attended the discovery and
exploration of the far places of the earth, blazed trails in
the wilderness, helped to open new continents, modified
or abolished the barbarisms of a thousand frontiers. It
has tempered the spirit of hatred and the lust to kill and
steal with a desire for mercy and a passion to help. It
has made the prison more of an institution of humane
reform and less a den of brutal punishment, and it has
handed down to us the modern hospital. It has humanized, if that be possible, the fierce methods of warfare,
made for amity and good-will among nations, given us
a code of international law. It has purified and improved the moral codes of every age and generation,
outlawed fear and given hope. It has been the author
of liberty and the sentinel of freedom. Men, who have
been the mere mechanics in the building of this vast
scheme, have often mislaid the plans, or lost their vision,
or blundered terribly in their work. Yet the building
has gone on, and the plan of the Mighty Architect is
slowly working out.

Christianity rests! But no, Christianity can never
rest. The marching of the Eleven is never done. The

Christian is enlisted in a war that knows no armistice, that admits of no discharge. We can ill afford to spend any time in bowing to the past while all about us are bugles calling to new action. Society, influenced profoundly though it has been by the Christian ethic and spirit, is not yet Christian, nor is it a just order. A few privileged ones amass and hoard the wealth of the land while the longest bread-lines in history form outside our doors. We spend a thousand dollars a minute on preparation for war while we preach the "Prince of Peace." We burn men out in the fiery furnaces of a new mechanized industry and throw them on the human scrap-heap before they reach forty years of age, in direct contradiction to the emphasis of Jesus on the sacredness of human personality and the ultimate value of human life. No, society is not yet Christian, and there is much to convince us that the Kingdom is not yet. But where should we be had Jesus never come? He has built a better world. The Eleven who were told to "go . . . and teach all nations, baptizing them," have made life more abundant. Those who labor to-day, who shall labor after us, to-morrow, to establish a world-order of justice, mercy and peace in place of the present order of hatred, fear and conflict, *shall* build a still better world beneath the hand of Him whose last promise is still the inspiration of advance: "Lo, I am with you always, even unto the end of the world."

INDEX

INDEX